A PRODUCTIVITY P

AN INTERACTIVE COURSE OF STUDY THAT EMPOWERS HOSPITAL MANAGERS
TO TAKE CONTROL OF THEIR DEPARTMENTS' LABOR PRODUCTIVITY AND
TALK LIKE AND WITH THEIR CHIEF FINANCIAL OFFICER

KEITH J. GOTT

First printing March 2010

ISBN 978-0-9844096-0-0

Title page picture: This symbol is used by the Ordnance Survey and other surveyors to pinpoint an exact height above sea level, which is denoted by the horizontal line above the arrow. This provides the standard, "Benchmark," from which all other heights are measured. © Copyright Andrew Stuart and licensed for reuse under this Creative Commons License

IMPORTANT

The purchase of this workbook entitles you to access our web-based Productivity Practicum testing site at no additional cost. There are two tests for each participant — one PRIOR to using the workbook and another AFTER completing the workbook. The tests tests are a tool to aid senior management in measuring value, progress, and areas requiring additional focus.

Send an email to Testing@ahs-c.com, noting 1) Your name and title, 2) the name of your institution, 3) the number of persons taking the tests and 4) the timeframe in which the tests will be taken (beginning and ending dates).

The URL of the testing site, and instructions, will then be emailed to your attention.

The results will then be analyzed and a summary report of results and findings will be emailed to your attention within five working days of the above-referenced ending date.

Book edited and cover designed by RootSky Books (A RootSky Creative company)
www.rootskybooks.com I www.rootskycreative.com

Contents

this page intentionally left blank

Preface

I have been working with hospital department managers to improve their departments' efficiency and effectiveness for more than twenty years. While much of that was one-on-one, I've also taught innumerable classes on the subject of labor productivity management and how to apply the concepts.

Whether teaching managers at a Critical Access Hospital in rural Iowa or teleconferencing with a dozen hospitals in the Pacific Northwest, I believe an interactive experience is critical. It's important to apply the concepts learned in the class — right there in the class. I randomly call on participants ("my victims") to provide their answers. Sometimes I spot one or more sitting there, glaring at me. They <u>are not</u> happy to be in the class. They <u>are not</u> comfortable with the subject. They <u>are</u> good clinicians; they just don't understand labor productivity and they're tired of the "bean counters" telling them their department is off target and making them feel like bad managers. You guessed it — they <u>are</u> my favorite challenges.

When someone greets me with a scowl, I redouble my efforts, because there are few things more enjoyable than watching the transformation as they participate in the exercises, answer my queries, and apply the concepts. This is the same spirit with which I wrote this "Productivity Practicum" workbook.

prac·ti·cum
Pronunciation: \prak-ti-kəm\
Function: noun
Etymology: German Praktikum, from Late Latin practicum,
neuter of practicus practical

: a course of study designed especially for the preparation of teachers and clinicians that involves the practical application of previously studied theory

By permission. From Merriam-Webster's Collegiate® Dictionary, 11th Edition ©2010 by Merriam-Webster, Incorporated (www.Merriam-Webster.com).

This workbook is fashioned with one goal in mind: to work with hospital department managers and directors to revisit the terms and concepts they've been hearing for years, practice applying those concepts, and show them how to change from "victims of productivity," into "drivers of productivity."

Like my classes and seminars, this workbook is a hands-on experience, offering practical exercises for line managers. Review points and/or exercises follow key chapters. The exercises are organized into three sections: Easy, Moderate and Challenging. The idea is to dig progressively deeper into the reviewed concepts.

If you wish to read a higher level book, oriented toward senior management, I highly recommend an excellent book by Paul Fogel, CEO of Executive Information Systems, titled *"Superior Productivity in Healthcare Organizations: How to Get It, How to Keep It."*

1. Introduction

Labor productivity management is not an art, nor is it a dark art. Labor productivity management is a science, but it is not rocket science. There are consistent concepts, definitions, calculations and tools that only differ in their application, clarity of presentation and consistency of accountability.

This Productivity Practicum seeks to:

1) Revisit the fundamentals of labor productivity management.

2) Dispel misunderstandings about hospital labor productivity.

3) Enable department managers to apply these concepts, so they <u>can</u> "talk like and with the Chief Financial Officer" and his or her staff about their department's productivity and labor requirements.

4) Support Senior Management's efforts to inculcate labor productivity management into the organization, so it becomes a natural part of hospital management and not some uncomfortable, episodic and even arcane topic revisited only in times of current or forecasted peril.

2. Environment

Government programs directly cover 28 percent of the U.S. population, including the elderly, disabled, children, veterans, and some of the poor. Programs include Medicare, Medicaid, SCHIP (State Children's Health Insurance Program) and the Veteran's Administration. Public spending accounts for 45 to 56 percent of health care spending. [1]

In 2007, 45.7 million people in the U.S. (15.3 percent of the population) were without health insurance for at least part of the year. The costs of treating the uninsured must often be absorbed by providers as "charity care", passed on to the insured via cost shifting and higher health insurance premiums, or paid by taxpayers through higher taxes. [2]

The federal government enacted EMTALA (the Emergency Medical Treatment and Active Labor Act) in 1986. It requires that hospital emergency departments treat emergency conditions of all patients regardless of their ability to pay. However, the government established no direct payment mechanism for such care. More than half of all emergency care in the U.S. is uncompensated. [3] This unfunded mandate has further contributed to financial pressures on hospitals.

Conclusion: Between government funded programs, private insurance providers that dictate reimbursement rates without regard to the actual cost of providing services to a patient, and uninsured patients who are unable or unwilling to pay for their services, hospitals have diminishing control over their revenues.

> Hospitals must wield strict control over their costs to generate sufficient funds for operational and capital requirements.

Labor is the number one operating expense for hospitals. More than fifty percent of operating expenses are associated with Salaries, Wages and Benefits paid to hospital staff.

Hospitals and Health Systems that create a "culture of productivity" by making efficiency and effectiveness a focus of their organization will see noteworthy results in their labor costs. In a culture of productivity, managers are taught how to manage their departments' labor productivity, given the tools to make it happen, and are held accountable and provided incentives for achieving appropriate, controllable goals.

Such organizations see higher manager morale than organizations where managers feel productivity demands are arbitrary and the reports and metrics they are provided, if they are provided at all, are in an indecipherable language.

Review:

1. Hospitals have diminishing control over their revenues.

2. The largest hospital operating expense is Salaries, Wages and Benefits.

3. Hospitals and Health Systems must create a "culture of productivity" in which managers are educated about labor productivity management, provided the necessary tools to monitor and impact their departmental productivity, and are held accountable and provided incentives for achieving efficiency and effectiveness targets.

Notes

3. Productivity Terms and Concepts

Note: The terms and concepts that are discussed in this chapter are presented in a cumulative fashion. The goal is to "layer" information, such that subsequent terms and concepts build on previously introduced ones.

In economics, "productivity" is the amount of output (in terms of goods produced or services rendered) per unit of input. Labor productivity is typically measured as output per employee or output per labor-hour.

Labor productivity is measured in productive hours per unit of service, calculated by the formula:

$$\frac{\text{Total Productive Hours}}{\text{Volume of Unit of Service}}$$

Hours and Other Staffing Measures

Productive Hours — These are hours deemed to be "manager controllable", including Regular and Overtime hours. Non-productive and call hours are excluded. Call-back hours are considered a form of overtime hours in most payroll systems.

For the purposes of benchmarking (see *Chapter 6. Benchmarking — Where Do I Stand?*), Education and Orientation hours are also included as "productive" time. While effective arguments can be made for excluding these from manager controllable time, the major benchmark database vendors include these in their productive hours.

PRODUCTIVE HOURS						
Regular	Overtime	Education	Orientation			

Note: If your hospital's senior management prefers to exclude education and orientation hours from calculated productive time, department benchmark metrics should be comparably adjusted to net out education and orientation time.

Non-Productive Hours — These include time paid for Vacation, Holiday and Sick time (or PTO if consolidated as Paid Time Off) as well as Jury or Bereavement Leave hours.

				NON-PRODUCTIVE HOURS		
				PTO/Holiday	Jury	Bereavement

Total Paid Hours — Combining Total Productive and Total Non-Productive hours yields Total Paid Hours.

TOTAL PAID HOURS						
Regular	Overtime	Education	Orientation	PTO/Holiday	Jury	Bereavement

Note: On-call or shift differential hours are excluded from all labor productivity calculations, but their expenses should be included in Total Labor Cost metrics (see Chapter 4. Calculating your Productivity).

Paid-to-Productive Ratio — This ratio is simply the division of actual Total Paid Hours by Total Productive Hours ("Worked Hours") for a given period. This ratio is used in calculating Target Paid Hours, for a period, by adjusting Target Productive Hours by the Paid-to-Productive Ratio for that period. For example:

If Bev Spangler's department shows 117,936 Paid Hours, and 103,784 Productive Hours, for the past year, her department's Paid to Productive Ratio would be calculated as:

117,936 Paid Hours / 103,784 Productive Hours = 1.136 Paid:Productive

If Target Productive Hours for the year totaled 118,200, then Bev's Target Paid Hours would be translated as:

118,200 Productive Hours x 1.136 Paid:Productive = 134,275 Target Paid Hours

FTE — Full-Time Equivalent is abbreviated as "FTE." The number of FTEs is calculated by dividing the Total Paid or Productive hours by a figure based on the length of the review period. Examples include:

One Week	40 hours	
Pay Period	80 hours	2 weeks at 40 hours per week
One Year	2080 hours	52 weeks at 40 hours per week
One Month	173.3 hours	2080 hours per 12 months

If a department's productive hours totaled 2,208, in the most recent pay period, their FTEs would be calculated as:

2,208 Productive Hours / 80 Hours per Pay Period = 27.6 Productive FTEs

Using Bev's department numbers above, we can calculate her Productive and Paid FTEs.

103,784 Productive Hours / 2,080 Hours per Year = 49.9 Productive FTEs

117,936 Paid Hours / 2,080 Hours per Year = 56.7 Paid FTEs

Note: Some hospitals convert Worked FTEs to equivalent Paid FTEs by dividing productive hours by a number that assumes a given non-productive rate. For example, they may divide annual productive hours by 1,840 (implies 11.5% non-productive as a percent of paid time) to create an equivalency to Paid FTEs. This applies a plugged Paid-to-Productive rate to actual department results. In this workbook, Worked FTEs and Paid FTEs will be calculated per the same period-appropriate denominators (see list above).

Fixed Staffing — Certain departments or staff are not expected to flex staffing relative to changing volumes. These departments or staff are referred to as "Fixed." Some hospitals or health systems have a policy of no fixed departments. In such instances, every department flexes. Staff in overhead departments may take a PTO day if hospital volume indicators, such as the inpatient census, drop below a certain level.

In the graph titled "Fixed", below, targeted staffing levels (vertical axis) <u>do not change</u> as the volume (horizontal axis) increases or declines.

Variable Staffing — Most hospital departments have variable staffing targets. They are assigned a staffing standard for each monitored volume unit of service. The departmental productivity target is the result of multiplying the review period volume by the variable staffing standard.

In the graph titled "Variable", below, targeted staffing levels <u>directly change</u> relative to department volume's increase or decline. This relationship is represented by the diagonal dotted line. Key volume points, and their associated staffing target, are represented by the grey vertical lines that connect the volume to the associated target.

Core Staffing — Core Staffing, also known as "Minimum Staffing" is the amount of staff required if there was only one unit of patient service to be delivered on a shift: one Patient Day, one Patient Meal, one Laboratory Test, etc. This is the "floor" for flexing down a department.

In the middle graph, below, the diagonal line does not intersect at volume <u>and</u> staff = zero. Rather, this example assumes Core Staffing at volume at or approaching zero. The rightmost graph, below, displays the relationship between volumes and targeted staffing levels for a department with mixed (Fixed & Variable) standards. In this example, too, Core Staffing is assumed as volume approaches zero.

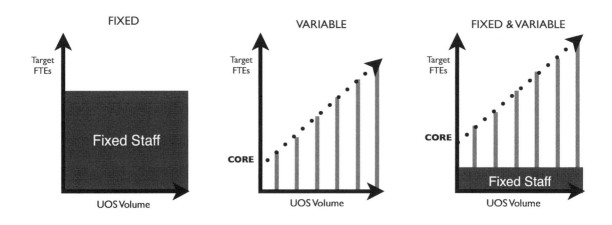

Review:

1. Labor productivity targets, and results, are measured in Productive Hours per Unit of Service.

2. For most labor productivity benchmarking databases, Productive Hours include Regular, Overtime , Education and Orientation hours.

3. For most labor productivity benchmarking databases, Paid Hours include Productive Hours plus PTO (or Vacation, Holiday and Sick — if broken out), Jury and Bereavement Leave hours.

4. FTE stands for Full Time Equivalent. The industry standard for one FTE is 80 hours per 14-day pay period, 2080 hours per year, or approximately 173 hours per month.

Volume Measures

Units of Service — A department's measure of work volume is referred to as a Unit of Service (or "UOS"). The units of service generally correspond to those used in the hospital's chosen benchmarking database (refer to vendor documentation for details regarding definitions and what is included or excluded in the volume computations). For nursing departments, the UOS is typically Patient Days, for Laboratory the UOS is Billed Tests, for Dietary it is Meal Equivalents, etc. Department productivity targets can be based on two or more units of service. For example, an Emergency Department may have different targets for Emergency Visits versus Fast Track Visits.

Weighted Units of Service — Some units of service may be weighted. In weighting a unit of service, the majority of a department's work volume measures will have a weight of 1.0, the norm, and certain department work measures will be higher or lower, representing the proportional demand on staff to provide that particular service. In such a scenario, if one service unit has a weight (or Relative Value) of 1.0, then another with a weight of 3.0 requires approximately three times the duration and staff intensity.

One example of this is in Physical Therapy. Most Physical Therapy treatments are charged in 15-minute units. However, if an evaluation requires one hour, the charge is <u>one unit</u> of CPT code 97001 (Physical Therapy Evaluation). If a subsequent reevaluation of the patient (97002) takes one-half hour, one unit is still charged. Patient evaluations and reevaluations charge units do not reflect the time required.

Rather than use "procedures" as a UOS, department managers may prefer to use weighted units of service — keeping their volumes in "15-minute equivalents." In the example above, an evaluation would be weighted at four units and a reevaluation would be weighted at two for productivity purposes. Any procedures still charging in 15-minute increments are assigned a productivity volume weighting of one.

Equivalent Patient Days — A nursing unit's standard unit of service is Patient Days. This figure is derived from the hospital's billing system (the Midnight Census). The metric does not take into consideration movement within the unit throughout the day: patients admitted to and discharged from the unit and patients cared for on an outpatient (or observation) basis.

While there is no standard mechanism for giving nursing units credit for admit and discharge activity, the Equivalent Patient Day is a rough effort to give credit for outpatient or observation activity. On units, where outpatient stays are tracked based on hours, Total Outpatient Hours are collected for the review period, divided by 24, and added to Patient Days for the same unit — the combination is total Equivalent Patient Days.

For example:

> Inpatient Nursing Department 6020 has 252 Patient Days in a pay period (Avg. Daily Census = 18). In that same pay period they provide 504 hours of on-unit outpatient observation support.
>
> 504 hours translates to 21 Equivalent Patient Days (504/24).
>
> For the period, their volume will be: 252 Patient Days + 21 Equivalent Patient Days = **273 Equivalent Patient Days**

Adjusted Patient Days and Adjusted Discharges — These factors are a measure of proximate scale of hospital operations. They are used to measure hospital-wide labor productivity as well as that of administrative departments such as Information Technology, Accounting, and Finance and Administration.

First, the Adjustment Factor is calculated for the review period. The formula for the adjustment factor is:

$$\frac{\text{Gross Inpatient and Outpatient Revenues}}{\text{Gross Inpatient Revenues}}$$

The result will typically be in the 1.5 to 3.0 range.

Next, the adjustment factor is multiplied by the Adult & Pediatric Patient Days for the review period, to achieve Adjusted Patient Days. Similarly, multiplying Adult & Pediatric Discharges by the adjustment factor will yield Adjusted Discharges.

Adjusted Occupied Beds — Also referred to as AOB's or Adjusted Daily Census, Adjusted Occupied Beds are calculated by dividing the Adjusted Patient Days for the review period by the number of days in that review period. AOBs are used as a denominator in the hospital-level metric FTEs per AOB. Total Hospital Paid FTEs are divided by AOBs for comparison to operating targets, prior period actual results, and to peer hospitals.

For example, Southeast Rural Hospital had an Adjustment Factor of 1.89 and 12,045 Total Patient Days in the most recent year. Adjusted Occupied Beds, or Adjusted Daily Census, for the year are calculated as:

(12,045 Patient Days / 365 Days) = 33.0 Average Daily Census

33.0 Average Daily Census x 1.89 Adjustment Factor = **62.4 AOBs**

Review:

1. Labor productivity targets and results are typically measured in Productive Hours per Unit of Service.

2. Units of Service, or UOS, is a name for a department's designated work measure for volume of services provided.

3. Some productivity units of service are weighted. Some examples include Physical Therapy, Occupational Therapy and Speech Therapy 15-minute equivalent measures and AARC Respiratory Therapy Clinical Activity Time Standard and Relative Weight measures.

4. The Equivalent Patient Day calculation is used by some hospitals to give nursing units credit for outpatient or observation activity.

5. Department productivity targets can be based on two or more units of service.

6. Adjusted Patient Days, Adjusted Occupied Beds and Adjusted Discharges are measures of proximate scale of hospital operations. They are used to measure hospital-wide labor productivity as well as that of some administrative departments.

EXERCISE 3.1   (Easy)

3.1.1   Labor Productivity is measured in:

    a.   Total Paid FTEs as a percent of Budgeted FTEs.

    b.   Staff per Facility Patient Day.

    c.   Productive hours per Unit of Service.

    d.   None of the above.

3.1.2   Productive Hours, also often referred to as Worked Hours, are typically a combination of:

    a.   Regular Hours, Overtime Hours and On-call Hours

    b.   Regular Hours, Overtime Hours, On-call Hours and Contract Labor hours

    c.   Regular Hours, Overtime Hours, Contract Labor Hours and Education/ Orientation hours.

    d.   Regular Hours and Contract Labor hours.

3.1.3   A department's productivity report shows 3,460 Worked Hours in the most recent pay period. How many Worked FTEs ("Productive FTEs") is this?

3.1.4   The Laboratory department has a productivity target of 0.175 Worked Hours per Billed Test. Calculate the department's Target Worked Hours for a pay period when the volume was 20,000 Billed Tests.

3.1.5   Referring to the information in 3.1.4: The department's actual Worked Hours totaled 3,360. What was the actual Worked Hours per Billed Test for the period?

3.1.6   What is the ADC for a nursing unit with 316 Patient Days in a pay period?

3.1.7   Department 6023 had a volume of 11,315 Patient Days in the previous year. In the same period, staff worked 105,230 hours (productive time). What were the Total Hours per Patient Day (HPPD) for the period?

3.1.8   Department 6024 had 273 Patient Days in the most recent pay period. If their productivity target (staffing standard) is 7.76 Worked Hours per Patient Day (HPPD), how many Target Worked FTEs do they have for the period?

EXERCISE 3.2   (Moderate)

3.2.1   Equivalent Patient Days are:

   a.   The combination of a nursing unit's patient days and admissions.

   b.   Designed to give nursing units some credit for observation activity

   c.   The combination of a nursing unit's patient days and observation hours/24

   d.   All of the above.

   e.   b and c.

3.2.2   Adjusted Patient Days and Adjusted Discharges are:

   a.   Generally used as a denominator, reflecting a hospital's scale of services. Hospital-wide or support departments' FTEs then divided by Adjusted Patient Days or Adjusted Discharges, to show their size in relationship to the scale of services supported.

   b.   Hospital Total Inpatient Adult and Pediatric Days, or Discharges, multiplied by an adjustment factor that gives credit for labor demands associated with out-patient activity.

c. a and b.

d. none of the above.

3.2.3 Using the data provided in 3.1.3, Non-Productive Hours were 12% of Productive hours for the pay period. What was the department's Total Paid Hours for that pay period?

3.2.4 Using the results from 3.2.3, What was the department's total Paid FTEs?

EXERCISE 3.3   (Challenging)

3.3.1 An ICU has a Core Staffing level of two nurses around the clock.
       How many Worked (Productive) FTEs does that equate to?

3.3.2 MidWest Community Hospital's Outpatient Physical Therapy Department has the schedule, below, for the next pay period:

Monday — Friday
        1 - Manager (8 hrs/day)
        4 - Physical Therapists (8 hrs/day)
        2 - Physical Therapy Assistants (8 hrs/day)
        1 - Clerk (8 hrs/day)

Saturday
        2 - Physical Therapists (8 hrs/day)
        1 - Clerk (8 hrs/day)

Sunday (closed)

How many Worked FTEs have been scheduled for the pay period?

3.3.3   MidWest Community Hospital had 120,450 Adjusted Patient Days, and 1,617 Paid FTEs this past year, what is their Paid FTEs per AOB?

3.3.4   Using the results from 3.1.4, if Non-Productive Hours equal 9% of Productive, for the reviewed period, what is the Total Target Paid Hours for that period?

3.3.5   Using the results from 3.3.4, how many Paid FTEs does that equate to?

3.3.6   The 3 East Medical Unit recorded 744 Patient Days and 2,604 Observation Hours for the month of December. What was their Equivalent Patient Days total for the month?

3.3.7   The OB/Gyn Unit recorded 224 Patient Days and 336 Observation Hours for the month of February. What was their Equivalent Patient Days total for the month?

3.3.8   MidWest Community Hospital shows $814 million in Total Charges (Gross Patient Revenues) for the year. Of that, $472 million is Inpatient Charges. What is the resulting Adjustment Factor?

3.3.9   Using the Adjustment Factor in 3.3.8, and the Adjusted Patient Days in 3.3.3, what was the Average Daily Census for the hospital that year?
[please round to the nearest Day]

3.3.10 Referring to 3.3.3: If the hospital's global staffing target is 4.75 Paid FTEs per AOB, how many FTEs are they away from their target?
[please round to the nearest FTE]

Notes

Notes

unit of service - Pt days)

4. Calculating Productivity

Types of Hours used in Calculating Labor Productivity Measures

As you will recall, from *Chapter 3. Productivity Terms and Concepts*, **Productive (Worked) Hours** are defined as including: Regular, Overtime, Contract Labor, Education and Orientation Hours. Education and Orientation Hours are typically included in Productive Hours by the major labor productivity benchmark vendors.

Contract Labor — Contract Labor can be defined as: non-payroll staff paid in lieu of payroll labor. This may include Nurse Agency and Traveler staff, contracted interim managers, and temporary workers. This also includes outsourced management of Dietary, Housekeeping, Plant and Engineering, Laundry or Pharmacy departments.

Non-Productive Hours — Vacation, Sick, Holiday, Jury Leave, Bereavement Leave are all considered non-productive time.

Paid Hours — Paid Hours include both Productive and Non-Productive Hours.

Call Hours and Differential Hours — are <u>not</u> included in any productive hours calculations. However, their <u>costs</u> should be included when monitoring overall labor expenses such as: Total Labor Expenses, Total Labor Expense Per Hour, or Total Labor Expense Per Unit of Service.

Labor Productivity Targets

Staffing Standards, another name for labor productivity targets, are typically measured in Worked Hours per Unit of Service. The staffing standard is the building block for calculating department labor productivity targets .

The steps for calculating target productive hours and FTEs, are:

1. Staffing Standard x Period Volume = Target Worked (Productive) Hours

2. Target Worked Hours / period Hours per FTE = Target Worked FTEs

3. Target Worked FTEs x Actual Paid-to-Productive Ratio = Target Paid FTEs

> Staffing Standards may be equal to or derived from benchmarks, engineered productivity targets or department operating budgets.

Single Staffing Standard

MidWest Community Hospital's CT Department has a staffing standard of 0.70 Worked Hours per Procedure. For the most recent pay period, the department volume was 490 procedures (50 per day). Total Worked and Paid Hours for the period were 333 and 360, respectively. The department's Targets are calculated at:

0.70 Worked Hours per Procedure x 490 Procedures =
343 Worked Hours

343 Worked Hours / 80 Hours per FTE = **4.3 Target Worked FTEs**

4.3 Target Worked FTEs x (360/333) = **4.6 Target Paid FTEs**

Once again, Actual Worked (Productive) Hours were 333 for the period. This is less than the target (343 Worked Hours) so the department's performance was favorable for the period. Calculating Actual Worked and Paid FTEs yields:

333 Worked Hours / 80 Hours per FTE = **4.2 Actual Worked FTEs**

360 Paid Hours / 80 Hours per FTE = **4.5 Actual Paid FTEs**

Multiple Staffing Standards

The process is very similar for departments with more than one staffing standard. Target worked hours are calculated for each unit of service. The target worked hours are then "pooled" into a Combined Worked Hours Target for the department for the period.

(Staff. Standard Procedure A) x (Volume Procedure A) = Target Worked Hours A

(Staff. Standard Procedure B) x (Volume Procedure B) = Target Worked Hours B

Target Worked Hours A + Target Worked Hours B =**Total Target Worked Hours**

For example, Southeast Rural Hospital has a Medical/Surgical Unit that also supports Pediatric patients. The department has staffing standards for both Med/Surg Patient Days (9.0 Worked Hours/Patient Day) and Pediatric Patient Days (14.0 Worked Hours per Patient Day). Over the past year, department volumes totaled 6,570 Med/Surg Patient Days and 1,460 Pediatric Patient Days (Combined = 8,030 Patient Days). Actual staffing measures for the period were 85,280 Worked Hours and 94,660 Paid Hours.

6,570 Med/Surg Patient Days x 9.0 Worked Hours per Patient Day =
59,130 Target Worked Hours

1,460 Pediatric Patient Days x 14.0 Worked Hours per Patient Day =
20,440 Target Worked Hours

59,130 + 20,440 = **79,570 Total Target Worked Hours**

79,570 Target Worked Hours / 2080 Worked Hours per FTE =
38.3 Target Worked FTEs

38.3 Target Worked FTEs x (94,660/85,280) = **42.5 Target Paid FTEs**

Actual Worked (Productive) Hours were 85,280 for the year. This is more than the 79,570 target, so the department's performance was **un**favorable.

The productivity report for this period might summarize the target as 9.90 Worked Hours per Total Patient Days (Total Worked Hours/(Combined Med/Surg plus Pediatric Patient Days)). The next period, the summarized target will probably be different due to a changing mix of Med/Surg vs. Pediatric Patient Days.

Note: It's important to remember that the period-by-period patient mix is driving the changing <u>summary</u> standard. The individual Target Worked Hours per Patient Day drivers do not change.

Fixed and Variable Productivity Targets

As noted above, certain departments or staff are not expected to flex staffed hours relative to changing volumes. These departments or staff are referred to as "Fixed." These departments are still accountable for achieving their staffing targets.

Most service delivery departments have variable staffing targets. They are assigned a staffing standard for one or more units of service. However, some hospitals employ both Fixed and Variable staffing targets for their service delivery departments. In this case, each period's staffing target is a combination of the fixed and calculated variable components.

For example, Department 6012 has a staffing standard comprised of 2.0 FTEs of Fixed Staff (Manager and Clerk: 72 hours of productive and 8 hours non-productive time per pay period each) and a variable standard of 8.00 Worked Hours per Patient Day (HPPD).

If the department has 378 Patient Days in a pay period (ADC=27), their productivity target will be calculated as Fixed + Variable = Total.

> Fixed = 2 Staff x 72 Hours per Pay Period each = **144 hours**
>
> Variable = 378 Patient Days x 8.00 HPPD = **3,024 Worked Hours**
>
> Total Target Worked Hours = 144 + 3,024 = **3,168 Worked Hours**

The productivity report for this department might summarize the target as 8.38 Worked Hours per Patient Day (3,168 Worked Hours/378 Patient Days). The next period, the summarized target will likely be different, due to a changing mix.

For example, if the volume is 393 Patient Days, in the next period, that period's target will be calculated as:

Fixed = 2 Staff x 72 Hours per Pay Period each = **144 hours**

Variable = 393 Patient Days x 8.00 HPPD = **3,144 hours**

Total Target Worked Hours = 144 + 3,144 = **3,288 Worked Hours**

The productivity report would summarize the target as 8.36 Worked Hours per Patient Day (3,288 Worked Hours/393 Patient Days). Just as with the departments with multiple staffing standards (see above), the summarized standard simply reflects the changing mix — Fixed versus Variable.

"Static" vs. "Dynamic" Units of Service

There are two main types of units of service: "Dynamic" and "Static." Dynamic units of service are used for departments with variable demand volumes. Examples include: Patient Days, Emergency Department Visits, Laboratory Tests, Radiology Procedures, Surgery Cases, etc. These units of service are <u>cumulative</u>. For example, if your Emergency Department supports 125 Visits on Friday, 180 on Saturday and 165 on Sunday, you have supported 470 Visits over those three days.

Static Units of Service, as the name implies, don't change from day to day and are not cumulative. For example, the unit of service for Housekeeping is generally Square Feet Cleaned. This volume rarely changes, unless a unit is closed or opened. If the MidWest Community Hospital Environmental Services department cleans 400,000 square feet on Friday, Saturday and Sunday, their volume will be 400 Thousand Square Feet Cleaned, for three days, not 1200 Thousand Square Feet Cleaned. Other examples of static units of service include Square Feet Maintained, Square Feet Patrolled, Computer Nodes Supported, Hospital FTEs and Hospital Employees.

Some productivity reports and benchmark services use monthly staffing standards for static departments (these can be converted to bi-weekly). Some productivity standards work on the principle noted in the example above — multiplying a daily factor by the number of the days in the reporting period. When they do that, the staffing standard looks quite small. But remember, it's being multiplied by a larger volume.

High Level Summary Productivity Ratios

Some productivity reporting system vendors offer a quick summary measure to show favorable or unfavorable results for a period. This metric, or "Productivity Ratio" as it is called in this Practicum, is calculated as:

$$\frac{\text{Target Productive Hours}}{\text{Actual Productive Hours}}$$

If actual results are less than target (a favorable result), then the denominator will be less than the numerator and the ratio will be greater than one. Conversely, if actual results are greater than target (an <u>un</u>favorable result), then the denominator will be greater than the numerator and the ratio will be less than one.

This ratio is presented as a percentage, so a "0.90" result will be displayed as "90%" and a "1.10" result will be displayed as "110%."

Using figures from the *Single Standard* example, the ratio is calculated as:

343 Target Worked Hours / 333 Actual Worked Hours = **1.03 or 103%**

Using figures from the *Multiple Standard* examples, the ratio is calculated as:

79,570 Target Worked Hours / 85,280 Act. Worked Hours = **0.933 or 93%**

The easiest way to remember which is the better result is to recall, "What score did we want in school — 79 percent or 95 percent?"

Note: In hospitals that include this useful metric in their productivity reports, some department managers <u>incorrectly</u> interpret it as their benchmark percentile performance (see Chapter 6. Benchmarking — Where Do I Stand?). This figure represents how well the department performed relative to hospital-designated productivity targets — which may or may not be based on benchmarks. A 79 percent summary productivity ratio indicates 79 percent of productivity target, not 79th percentile!

Review:

1. The "building block" for calculating labor productivity targets is the Staffing Standard (Target Worked Hours per Unit of Service).

2. Call Hours and Differential Hours are <u>not</u> included in labor productivity calculations, but their costs can be included when monitoring overall labor expenses such as Total Labor Expenses, Total Labor Expense Per Hour, or Total Labor Expense Per Unit of Service.

3. Most service delivery departments have variable staffing targets. They are assigned a staffing standard for one or more units of service.

4. For departments with more than one staffing standard, it's important to remember that the the <u>mix</u> of the units of service driving the overall worked hours target can change, so any resulting summary measure will change. However, the individual per UOS staffing standards do not change.

5. In many hospitals, certain departments or staff are not expected to flex staffed hours relative to changing volumes. These departments or staff are referred to as "Fixed."

6. "Static" Units of Service, as the name implies, do not change from day to day and are not cumulative. For example, the unit of service for Housekeeping is generally Square Feet Cleaned. This volume rarely changes, unless a unit is closed or opened.

EXERCISE 4.1   (Easy)

Fred Bachofen is the manager of MidWest Community Hospital's Laboratory Department. For the most recent two-week pay period, his productivity report shows:

Department Volume	25,000 Billed Tests
Regular Hours	3,995
Overtime Hours	243
Non-Productive Hours	470
Staffing Standard (Target)	0.165 Worked Hours per Billed Test (*doesn't Δ*)

4.1.1   What was Fred's department's average daily volume of Billed Tests?

4.1.2   How many Productive Hours did department staff work this pay period?

4.1.3   How many Paid Hours did department staff work this pay period?

4.1.4   How many Productive FTEs worked this pay period?

4.1.5   How many Paid FTEs did Fred's department have this period?

EXERCISE 4.2   (Moderate)

Using the data provided in Exercise 4.1:

4.2.1   What was the total Target Productive Hours for the most recent pay period?

4.2.2   What was the Actual Worked Hours per UOS for the pay period?

4.2.3   Was Fred's department's performance better or worse than target?

4.2.4   What was the resulting Productivity Ratio for the pay period?

EXERCISE 4.3   (Challenging)

Using the data provided in Exercise 4.1:

4.3.1   Given the same volume, how many fewer hours would Fred's staff have to work to achieve the Target Worked Hours per Billed Test?

4.3.2   How many billed tests would Fred's staff need to perform, with no additional hours, to achieve their productivity target?

4.3.3   What was the department's Non-Productive Hours as a Percent of Total Productive Hours for the period?

4.3.4   What was the department's Non-Productive Hours as a Percent of Total Paid Hours for the period?

EXERCISE 4.4   (Easy)

Sylvia Weber is the manager of 3 South — one of MidWest Community Hospital's Medical Surgical Units. For the most recent two-week pay period, her report shows:

Department Volume 1	385 Patient Days
Department Volume 2	252 Observation Hours
Regular Hours	3,244
Overtime Hours	198
Education/Orientation Hours	42
Non-Productive Hours	561
Staffing Standard (Target)	8.3 Worked Hours per Equiv. Patient Day

Note: All hours include all department staff.

4.4.1   What was the ADC for the unit for this pay period?

4.4.2   Please convert the Observation Hours to Equivalent Patient Days (EPDs)?

4.4.3   How many Total Equivalent Patient Days did 3 South staff support?

4.4.4   Excluding overtime hours, what was the Actual Worked Hours per Equivalent Patient Day?

4.4.5   What was the Total Worked Hours per Equivalent Patient Day?

4.4.6   How many Productive FTEs worked this pay period?

4.4.7   How many Paid FTEs did Sylvia's department have this period?

EXERCISE 4.5   (Moderate)

Using the data provided in Exercise 4.4:

4.5.1   What was the Target Productive Hours for the most recent pay period?

4.5.2   Was 3 South's performance better or worse than target?

4.5.3   What is the resulting Productivity Ratio for the pay period?

EXERCISE 4.6   (Challenging)

Using the data provided in Exercise 4.4:

4.6.1   Approximately how many FTEs of overtime did Sylvia utilize during
         the pay period?

4.6.2   What was the department's Non-Productive Hours as a Percent of Total
         Productive Hours for the period?

4.6.3   What was the department's Non-Productive Hours as a Percent of Total Paid
         Hours for the period?

EXERCISE 4.7   (Easy)

4.7.1   MidWest Community Hospital has contracted with a national firm to provide management for their Food and Nutrition department. True or False: these 3.0 FTEs are no longer included in the department's productivity report.

4.7.2   A hospital's Accounting department has a Fixed staffing target of 8.5 Paid FTEs. The most recent productivity report shows department staffing at 9.0 FTEs - down from 9.3 FTEs the prior year.

   a.   As the department is "Fixed", their actual productivity does not matter.

   b.   The department was staffed at 9.3 FTEs, last year, so they have improved. The current Fixed Target is not a troubling issue.

   c.   The department has a 0.5 Paid FTE unfavorable variance.

   d.   The department manager should assess department volume demands and revisit benchmarked staffing levels to see if there is justification for a periodic adjustment of the Fixed Target.

   e.   c and d

4.7.3   True/False: Departments with multiple staffing standards, or Fixed & Variable staffing standards, will see their summarized target (Worked Hours per Summary Unit of Service) change from period to period.

EXERCISE 4.8   (Moderate)

4.8.1   Which of the following units of service is <u>not</u> considered "static"?

  a. Square Feet Cleaned

  b. Devices Maintained

  c. Surgery Minutes

  d. Employees

4.8.2   True/False: Departments with static staffing standards are not included in hospital productivity reports.

4.8.3   A rural hospital provides both urgent and emergency care services in their Emergency Department. The department has separate staffing standards for each level of service: 2.50 Worked Hours per Emergency Visit and 1.20 Worked Hours per Urgent Care visit. The department's Summary Unit of Service is "Total Visits".

Department statistics for the most recent pay period show 562 Emergency Visits and 459 Urgent Care Visits. What was the department's overall Worked Hours per Visit target for the period?

4.8.4   Using the staffing standards in 4.8.3, if department statistics for the prior pay period showed 522 Emergency Visits and 399 Urgent Care Visits, what was the department's overall Target Worked Hours per Visit for the period?

4.8.5   Referring to 4.8.3 and 4.8.4, why did the Worked Hours per Visit target change from one pay period to the next?

EXERCISE 4.9   (Challenging)

4.9.1   MidWest Community Hospital's Laundry department processes approximately 2.2 million pounds of laundry per year. The department's productivity target is 1.45 Worked Hours per 100 pounds processed.

If the volume for the most recent month was 195,000 pounds, what was the department's target Worked FTEs?

4.9.2   Community Hospital of Sulphur Glen is building a replacement hospital facility. At 168,000 square feet, it is considerably larger than the old facility (129,000 sq.ft.). Mark Arnold, the Plant/Maintenance Manager, is preparing a budget for staffing the new facility. His current position control report shows 3.0 FTEs.

Mark's goal is to staff the department at the top quartile benchmark of 50.0 Worked Hours per Thousand Square Feet Maintained (annual). If the Paid-to-Productive ratio has been 1.12 for the past twelve months, approximately how many additional Paid FTEs will Mark request?

4.9.3   Painted Hills Memorial Hospital employs a combined Fixed/Variable productivity staffing standard. The Food and Nutrition department's productivity target includes 2.0 Fixed Paid FTEs, for the manager and one assistant. The department's variable target is 0.15 Worked Hours per Meal Equivalent (a unit of service that combines patient meals with equivalents calculated from cafeteria sales, nutritional supplements, etc.).

The department's Meal Equivalent volume totaled 11,814 in the most recent pay period. If the Paid-to-Productive ratio for the period was 1.09, what was the resulting Total Paid Hours target? How many Paid FTEs is that?

Notes

Notes

5. Position Control versus Productivity

It is not unusual for a department manager, when asked if they have a recent productivity report, to produce a copy of their Position Control report. While position control is a key part of labor management, it is not specifically a tool for managing labor productivity.

> Position Control reports show your available (payroll) labor resources.
> Productivity reports show how effectively you utilized those resources.

For example: Cathy Stuart is the manager of the Physical Therapy department at MidWest Community Hospital. When asked about her departmental productivity, she produces the report, below, and proclaims "I'm beating budget by nearly ten percent!" Can you see how she reached this conclusion?

DEPARTMENT POSITION CONTROL REPORT

CC Number	Job Code	Title	Grade	Budget FTEs	Actual FTEs
6450	127	Manager, Rehab Services	E13	1.0	1.0
6450	312	Physical Therapist - Team Leader	H11	1.0	1.0
6450	313	Physical Therapist	H10	1.0	1.0
6450	313	Physical Therapist	H08	2.0	2.0
6450	313	Physical Therapist	H07	2.0	2.0
6450	323	Physical Therapy Assistant	H05	3.0	2.0
6450	886	Clerk	C08	1.0	1.0
DEPARTMENT TOTAL - 6450 PHYSICAL THERAPY				**11.0**	**10.0**

Cathy currently has one of ten department positions open. But is she really "beating budget by nearly ten percent?" Looking at her productivity report (Exhibit 7.1), we see that Cathy has turned to registry staff and overtime utilization to make up her labor shortfall. When we look at her real productivity measures, she is actually performing worse than her target.

It is common to find organizations that monitor regular hours and wages yet exclude contract labor from productivity calculations. This offers an implicit reward for managers to utilize such "stealth manpower." The most effective productivity reports include these hours, as well as expenses, when reporting on departmental performance.

It's important to to revisit the fact the position control is one important component of labor management. Most hospitals have a Position Control Committee, comprised of members of Finance, Human Resources and Senior Management. Managers seeking to add staff must complete supporting documentation, showing they have available, budgeted positions.

However, not all hospitals require their managers to also show that they effectively utilize all of the staff they currently have. Requisition documents should also include current and year-to-date productivity results that show whether requesting managers are achieving their productivity targets. The committee can decide if they need to investigate further before they authorize adding any staff.

Review:

1. Position Control systems and reports are important tools in managing labor and productivity.

2. A Position Control system is not used for reporting labor productivity.

3. Position Control reports show the resources available to a department manager. Productivity reports show how effectively the manager utilizes those resources.

4. Position Control does not show Overtime or Contract Labor utilization in a department.

Notes

Notes

6. Benchmarking — Where Do I Stand?

Many hospitals only measure their progress by comparing their current performance to their own past performance. While there some discipline implicit in this action, it misses a key component — PERSPECTIVE.

> The story goes of two intrepid hunters who hired a bush pilot to ferry them into the Alaskan wild. To their delight, each bagged a sizable moose. When their pilot returned to bring them home, he goggled at the size of their trophies. "I can't bring both of those!" he exclaimed. "My Skywagon is only certified to carry 1,600 pounds — those two weigh nearly that all by themselves!!!" The hunters complained, cajoled and threatened him with no result. Finally, they resorted to bribery. He reluctantly agreed. Leaving the camping gear and equipment behind, the pilot taxied and started his ascent. He struggled to gain altitude and, inevitably failing, crashed into a distant stand of birch. As the three survivors struggled away from the wreckage, one hunter turned to the other and queried, "Where did we come down?" The other replied, "About a mile from where we crashed last year!"
>
> Remember, it's ALL about perspective...

It is critical to incorporate <u>peer performance</u> into the discipline of measuring hospital and department quality, productivity and cost performance. Otherwise, when you simply compare yourself, to yourself, you may fall prey to the axiom "the fastest way to fall behind is to stand still."

We are all familiar with the term "benchmarking." When I performed an internet search of the term, back in 1995, the number of "hits" was about 40,000. A recent search yielded over 50,000,000 hits!

One example of benchmarking is the growth charts children are measured against during their progression. Each visit, the pediatrician reports "Kristin is doing just fine — she's at the 55th percentile of her age group" or "Johnny's going to be a linebacker when he grows up — he's at the 93rd percentile!"

Where do benchmarks come from? Once again, it's science but not rocket science. Data points are collected for a given period (perhaps quarterly or annually), segregated into peer groups (for example: age group, school grade, Hospital Bed Size, NICU or Clinical Laboratory department, etc.) then scrubbed and sorted.

In the case of labor productivity, a dataset of comparable departments is collected and sorted from low to high. It's sorted in this fashion because a lower Worked Hours per Unit of Service measure is the stated goal. One quarter of the way down is the Top Quartile, halfway down is the Median (50th percentile) and three-quarters of the way down is the Bottom Quartile.

Some benchmark database vendors refer to the top quartile as the "75th percentile" and others as the "25th percentile." Likewise, depending on their approach, they will refer to the result one-tenth of the way down the list as either the "90th percentile" or the "10th percentile." Once your hospital selects a vendor, you adopt their syntax.

A	B	C	
8.82	6.99	6.99	
8.52	7.09	7.09	
6.99	7.15	7.15	
7.09	7.25	7.25	
8.52	7.40	7.40	
8.51	7.50	7.50	
9.02	8.09	8.09	Top Quartile
7.15	8.14	8.14	
8.49	8.29	8.29	
8.14	8.33	8.33	
8.71	8.33	8.33	
9.09	8.49	8.49	
8.09	8.51	8.51	
7.25	8.52	8.52	Median
10.11	8.52	8.52	
8.71	8.63	8.63	
8.33	8.71	8.71	
7.50	8.71	8.71	
8.29	8.71	8.71	
11.12	8.82	8.82	
8.33	8.90	8.90	Bottom Quartile
8.71	8.93	8.93	
8.63	8.94	8.94	
7.40	9.00	9.00	
8.90	9.02	9.02	
8.94	9.09	9.09	
8.93	10.11	10.11	
9.00	11.12	11.12	

In the exhibit, to the left, we see an unsorted list of 28 data points in the left column (column A). The data represents labor productivity results collected from a group of peer departments. The data are then sorted, in increasing order from top to bottom (column B). *Note: For benchmarking children's growth, as mentioned above, data points would be sorted in decreasing order as greater height is deemed more desirable.*

When the data have been reviewed and ordered, the percentiles can be identified (column C). For the Top Quartile, we simply mark the result one-quarter of the way down the list. In this case, the result is 8.09 Worked Hours per Unit Of Service. The Median result, also known as the 50th Percentile, the data point halfway down the dataset - 8.52. Remember, the median is the <u>midpoint,</u> not the <u>average,</u> of the range. The Lower Quartile of the range is three-quarters of the way down the sorted list - 8.90.

As noted earlier, benchmarks are also available for top and bottom deciles - these are the results one-tenth of the way from the top and the bottom. Depending on how the bench-marking service refers to them, these are the 90th Percentile or the 10th Percentile. In the case of the example above, reflecting the smaller sample size, the top decile would be 7.2 and the bottom decile would be 9.1.

Typical Benchmarking Practice

(see *Appendix: Typical Benchmarking Practice — Expanded* for further details).

Most healthcare facilities use the most basic form of benchmarking to measure their departmental efficiency as compared to "peer" departments. The process includes:

1. Select a review time period.

   a. Generally a year is used in order to eliminate seasonal variances.

2. Calculate departmental productivity, for the review period, by dividing the number of productive hours by the unit of service volumes. The resulting efficiency measure will be in units of Productive Hours per Unit of Service (also referred to as Worked Hours per Unit of Service).

3. Compare the resulting productivity measure to peer department results at key percentiles. Most hospitals look at the top decile, top quartile and median of the benchmarking database. Develop department performance targets based on achieving top quartile or top decile performance.

4. Many organizations stop at #3 — selecting staffing standards that are equal, or relative, to designated benchmarks. However, this is actually a beginning, not the end. This is a time for questions, not declarations. Managers should answer questions like:

   a. How are we different than our best performing peers?

   b. Are we constrained from improving our productivity measures due to:

      i. State mandates

      ii. Hospital administrative mandates

      iii. Significantly different patient demographics

      iv. Significantly different services

      v. Significantly different processes

      vi. Dated technology

      vii. Department's physical layout

Once the questions are answered, and the justified differences have been assessed for their measurable impact on efficiency ("justified" means they have survived the scrutiny and questions), the remaining difference from best practice peers must be addressed. The next step is to build an Action Plan, showing:

   1) Adjusted Staffing Targets

   2) What changes will be done to achieve those Targets

   3) What date they will be completed by and

   4) Who will be accountable for achieving the agreed-to targets.

Advanced Benchmarking Practices

(see *Appendix: Advanced Benchmarking Practice — Expanded* for further details).

According to Michael J. Spendolini, author of "The Benchmarking Book", "*Benchmarking is a continuos, systematic process of evaluating the products, services, and work processes of organizations that are recognized as representing best practices for the purposes of organizational improvement.*" [4]

> The most important thing to remember about benchmarking is
> Benchmarking is a beginning not an end.

Many organizations pursue expanded benchmarking and peering practices to seek opportunities and steps to improve their quality, efficiency and effectiveness.

These organizations undertake a full, systematic, ongoing process of designating teams to 1) investigate opportunities, 2) find best practice peers, 3) interview representatives of those peer hospitals and departments, 4) identify and implement process improvement opportunities, and 5) monitor and evaluate improved processes.

The Benchmarking Paradox — Who Keeps Moving the Target?

I participated in competitive swimming while growing up in California's Santa Clara Valley. For swimmers competing within the AAU (Amateur Athletic Union), there were benchmarks for each peer group — based on gender and ages. These benchmarks were titled "A" and "AA" Time Standards (the latter being more difficult to achieve than the former). Each season, we strove to achieve these lofty goals. Periodically, a new booklet would be published with updated A and AA times. And, as you can imagine, with each new publication, the times became more difficult to achieve.

Why was this? We imagined some "fat cats" with stogies gripped firmly in their teeth, working out ways to drive skinny little speedo-clad tykes mad. Not so. Each time, the database of swimmers' times was analyzed and the results at the designated performance percentiles identified. And... each time the benchmarks got a little faster...

So it is with productivity benchmarks...

> Think of it this way — **75**% of the participants are trying to squeeze into **25**% of the Real Estate!

Something has to give! Labor Productivity benchmarks are reassessed, periodically, based on <u>actual data</u>. The data is collected, scrubbed for anomalies, and analyzed for publication. While it is not a sure thing that a department's productivity targets will become more difficult to attain, from one year to the next, it is not unusual.

Review:

1. Too many hospitals measure their progress by only comparing their current performance to their own past performance.

2. At its most basic level, benchmarking is a mechanism for incorporating peer performance into the discipline of measuring departmental quality, efficiency and effectiveness.

3. Hospital labor productivity benchmarks reflect actual data from hospital and department peers.

4. Benchmarking is a beginning, not an end. It yields questions that can offer insights into managerial effectiveness and opportunities for improving operational quality, efficiency and effectiveness.

Notes

Notes

7. What's In Your Toolbox?

Overview

There are a number of important tools available to support managers' efforts to monitor and manage departmental productivity. These include:

    a.   Productivity reports (Daily, Bi-weekly or Monthly)

    b.   Staffing Grids (Daily or Shift)

    c.   Contract Labor Utilization reports

    d.   Time and Attendance reports

    e.   Labor Distribution Reports ("LDR")

    f.   Revenue and Usage reports

    g.   Monthly Manager's reports (Month and Year-to-Date Budget vs. Actual)

    h.   Position Control reports

Productivity Reports — Productivity reports are an obvious tool of choice for managing your departmental labor. These reports are most often provided on a bi-weekly or monthly basis. Many hospitals, that attempt to convert to a daily productivity report, find that their data collection can become a bottle-neck for accurate alignment of hours and volumes. Charging systems may be inaccurate due to delays with manually entered charges, pharmacy charge-backs and error corrections. Labor hours may be inaccurate due to any delays in Time and Attendance inputs and corrections. These "lags" are less of an issue with bi-weekly and monthly reports. Monthly reports are often criticized for failing to provide timely information. As one manager put it, "It's like the watchman on the Titanic saying 'What's with that iceberg a mile or so behind us?'"

See *Focus — Productivity Reports*, below, for further details.

Staffing Grids — Staffing Grids, also known as Staffing Matrices, are tools used by managers to align staffing to demand in a consistent, systematic manner. Not only do staffing grids offer the benefit of a coherent, consistent approach but, when variation from the plan is required, managers can make supporting notes for retrospective review. While Staffing Grids are a tool generally associated with inpatient nursing units, they are quite useful for <u>managers of any variable departments</u> with shifting client demands. See *Focus — Staffing Grids*, below, for further details.

While Productivity Reports and Staffing Grids seem like obvious tools for managing labor productivity, the other tools listed are also important.

> A key component of managing labor productivity is assessing the accuracy of the collected data used in all measurements.

Payroll Data — If your hospital has a Time & Attendance system, you will want to verify staff hours on a daily basis. Also, most hospital payroll systems have Labor Distribution Reports (LDRs). These reports show hours by employee (and classification) and key Pay Type categories (Regular, Overtime, Non-Productive, etc.) for the pay period or month.

Contract Labor Data — Contract labor hours and dollars information may be readily available from Accounting. If not, the information may be found in your Monthly Manager's Report (see *Financial Data* below). Many department managers keep their own records tracking Agency, Traveler and other contract labor time and expenses. These can be an excellent resource when verifying any Accounting reports.

Volume Data — The Revenue and Usage report shows volumes and dollars for charge items in your department. These reports can be run on a daily, bi-weekly or monthly basis. As volume is the denominator of the productivity performance metric, managers will want to verify that the charges are being captured correctly (and that any new service charges have been implemented).

Financial Data — Monthly Budget vs. Actual reports provided to department managers, often referred to as the "Monthly Manager's Reports", provide another opportunity to verify errors in labor costs assigned to your department. This may also be the only opportunity to verify contract labor dollars and, implicitly, contract labor hours assigned to your department. Since these reports are monthly, they will probably not agree with bi-weekly productivity reports due to accounting accruals. Nonetheless, they serve as another effective tool for catching possible errors.

Position Control — As stated earlier, Position Control is useful for assessing available labor resources, including total budgeted and actual staff positions, totals by job classification, Part-Time versus Full-Time, etc.

Focus — Productivity Reports

Note: Please refer to Exhibit 7.1 and 7.2 for descriptions below.

Most productivity systems provide reports in two formats: 1) a detailed report for each department and a 2) a summary report of department performance as compared to other hospital departments. I call the second format an "Embarrassment Report" as it often highlights best and worst performing departments. The latter report is generally for directors and senior management. Some hospitals provide both reports to their department managers.

Regardless of the format, an effective productivity report should show, for current and recent periods:

    a. Staffing Standard(s)

    b. Actual department volumes

    c. Target and Actual Productive (Worked) Hours and/or FTEs

    d. Target and Actual Paid Hours and/or FTEs

    e. Variance from targets

    f. Financial impact of missing (or beating) targets

The best reports allow a manager to quickly answer the question "How well did we do?" I call this "glance-ability". My definition of glance-ability is: the degree to which the reader can quickly determine how well the department performed, identify any trends or issues, and review supporting details.

In Exhibit 7.1, we see a sample productivity report for MidWest Community Hospital. The report is for bi-weekly time periods and displays details for 13 pay periods during a fiscal year, as well as the average results for the report-to-date. In the case of this sample report, the following categories of information are provided:

    a. Staffing Standard(s)

    b. Volumes(s)

    c. Hours - Target and Actual

    d. Hours per Unit of Service - Target and Actual

    e. FTEs Worked and Paid - Target and Actual

    f. Productivity Ratio

    g. Key Ratios

    h. Expense Summaries

    i. Financial Impacts

> One challenge for productivity reports, is to show useful information that doesn't become a featureless mosaic of numbers and characters that make one's head swim. Some fail this challenge.

In the report shown, the first line answers that most important question — "How did we do?." The Productivity Ratio concisely compares the period's target to actual productive hours (see *Chapter 3. Productivity Terms and Concepts*). Do <u>not</u> confuse this with benchmark percentiles — it does not represent the percentile at which the department is performing.

Volumes should be displayed for all units of service that drive the department's total target worked hours. Some departments have more than one unit of service, with associated staffing standards, all contributing to that department's total target worked (productive) hours. Managers should scrutinize this information for accuracy.

A variety of hours information will be provided: Target Worked Hours per Unit of Service, the staffing standard, is a fundamental piece of information — it drives most everything in the report. As we reviewed, above and in *Chapter 4. Calculating your Productivity*, a department may have more than one staffing standard. The staffing standard is multiplied by the volume of the associated units of service for each period to contribute to the target worked hours total for each period. Using your the information provided in your report, you should be able to make the same calculations and arrive at the same results.

Actual worked and paid hours should also be shown, for each period, with details provided including: Overtime, Contract Labor, Paid Time Off, and even Education and Orientation Time.

Actual paid hours, when divided by total worked (productive) hours yields the Paid-to-Productive ratio (see *Chapter 3. Productivity Terms and Concepts*). This ratio is then applied to the target worked hours for each period, resulting in target paid hours.

Rather than make you perform the calculation, most productivity reports will calculate the target vs. actual variance for metrics included in your reports. *Note: Statistically speaking, these are actually the difference between target and actual measures, but many hospital reports describe them as "variances".*

The most glance-able productivity reports offer graphical representation of key measures. With such graphs managers can quickly determine if there are any performance issues and then drill down using the detailed report. Exhibit 7.2 shows an example of how such a report might allow quick, useful feedback. Some productivity reports display key ratios, such as Overtime, Contract Labor and Non-Productive Percentages to help "red flag" areas of concern for department and senior managers.

MIDWEST COMMUNITY HOSPITAL
Productivity Report - PPE 05/04

Department: **6450 - Physical Therapy**
Units of Service **Timed Treatments**
Staffing Standard **0.45**

PERIOD	1/12	1/26	2/9	2/23	3/9	3/23	4/6	4/20	5/4	5/18	6/1	6/15	6/29	RPT AVG
PRODUCTIVITY														
Productivity Ratio	85%	81%	94%	87%	91%	88%	92%	89%	87%					88%
VOLUMES														
Timed Treatments	1,529	1,465	1,624	1,572	1,632	1,549	1,657	1,618	1,580					1,581
LABOR EXPENSE														
Labor $	18,766	19,089	18,768	19,649	19,888	19,736	19,812	20,185	20,050					19,549
HOURS														
Target Worked	688	659	731	707	734	697	746	728	711					711
Worked	812	809	777	812	805	794	812	814	813					805
Target Paid	757	734	796	785	825	791	823	809	781					789
Paid	893	900	846	901	904	901	896	904	893					893
Overtime	37	43	20	40	47	61	51	44	41					43
Contract/Agency	25	34	43	28	42	67	39	30	28					37
HOURS/UOS														
Target	0.45	0.45	0.45	0.45	0.45	0.45	0.45	0.45	0.45					0.45
Worked	0.53	0.55	0.48	0.52	0.49	0.51	0.49	0.50	0.51					0.51
Paid	1.23	1.32	1.54	0.99	1.13	1.04	1.19	1.10	1.25					1.20
FTES WORKED														
Target	8.6	8.2	9.1	8.8	9.2	8.7	9.3	9.1	8.9					8.9
Actual	10.2	10.1	9.7	10.2	10.1	9.9	10.2	10.2	10.2					10.1
Variance	1.5	1.9	0.6	1.3	0.9	1.2	0.8	1.1	1.3					1.2
FTES PAID														
Target	9.5	9.2	9.9	9.8	10.3	9.9	10.3	10.1	9.8					9.9
Actual	11.2	11.3	10.6	11.3	11.3	11.3	11.2	11.3	11.2					11.2
Variance	1.7	2.1	0.6	1.5	1.0	1.4	0.9	1.2	1.4					1.3
KEY RATIOS (PCT OF WKD)														
Non-Productive	10.0%	11.3%	8.9%	11.0%	12.3%	13.5%	10.4%	11.1%	9.9%					10.9%
Overtime	4.6%	5.3%	2.6%	4.9%	5.8%	7.7%	6.3%	5.4%	5.0%					5.3%
Contract/Agency	3.1%	4.2%	5.5%	3.4%	5.2%	8.4%	4.8%	3.7%	3.4%					4.2%
EXPENSE SUMMARIES														
Labor $/UOS	12.27	13.03	11.56	12.50	12.19	12.74	11.96	12.48	12.69					12.37
Labor Cost/Hr	21.01	21.20	22.18	21.80	22.00	21.90	22.10	22.32	22.44					21.88
$ Impact Prod	2,865	3,533	1,116	2,531	1,744	2,410	1,619	2,130	2,515					2,284
Prem. OT $	389	456	222	436	517	668	564	491	460					347

Exhibit 7.1

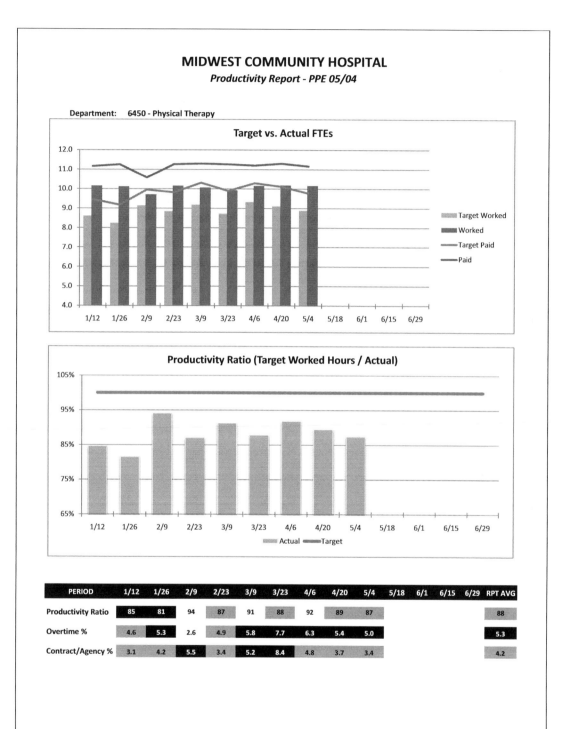

MIDWEST COMMUNITY HOSPITAL
Productivity Report - PPE 05/04

Department: 6450 - Physical Therapy

Target vs. Actual FTEs

- Target Worked
- Worked
- Target Paid
- Paid

Productivity Ratio (Target Worked Hours / Actual)

Actual — Target

PERIOD	1/12	1/26	2/9	2/23	3/9	3/23	4/6	4/20	5/4	5/18	6/1	6/15	6/29	RPT AVG
Productivity Ratio	85	81	94	87	91	88	92	89	87					88
Overtime %	4.6	5.3	2.6	4.9	5.8	7.7	6.3	5.4	5.0					5.3
Contract/Agency %	3.1	4.2	5.5	3.4	5.2	8.4	4.8	3.7	3.4					4.2

Exhibit 7.2

Focus — Staffing Grids

Productivity reports are rarely a surprise for some managers. They use staffing grids, spreadsheets and even notepads, to monitor and drive their department's labor performance.

Staffing grids, also known as staffing matrices, come in all shapes and sizes. The basic description of a staffing grid is a worksheet that models out staffing numbers and mixes at different volume levels. While most staffing grids are developed for inpatient units, I have worked with managers of all types of departments that support varying demand levels to implement such a tool.

The most important thing a staffing grid offers is <u>consistency</u>. The grids are developed with labor productivity targets in mind. If a manager follows the grid, she will meet her performance goals over time. Why not all the time? Even if she adheres to her staffing grid, she will probably not achieve departmental performance targets over <u>specific</u> periods. This is because of a key concept that many senior managers must remember:

STAFFING IS MODULAR, NOT LINEAR!

If you recall the three graphs, depicting fixed and variable staffing models, the two graphs of variable departments show a staffing target line that moves in a linear fashion relative to changes in growth.

But when a manager adds an additional employee on a shift, the productivity measure is immediately and negatively impacted. Conversely, using thoughtfully developed grids, managers respond to volume changes in a planned, consistent manner that delivers the desired efficiency and effectiveness. This is further addressed in *Chapter 8. Managing Productivity* (*Embrace the Volume*).

Exhibit 7.3 shows a basic staffing grid for a fictional nursing unit — 3 South Medical Surgical. The grid shows prescribed staffing mix and levels at various census levels —

by shift. Looking at the header we see that the unit has a capacity of 32 patients, a budgeted Average Daily Census of 20 and a Staffing Standard (Productivity Target) of 8.50 Worked Hours per Patient Day.

Looking at the left side of the grid we see census levels ranging from 8 to 32. Any census at or below 10 will be at "core" staffing levels (minimum staffing). If the census falls below 8, the unit may be closed and patients transferred to 3 North Medical.

Displayed to the right of the various staffing columns, are the total staffed hours associated with each of the census levels as well as the resulting productive hours per unit of service. In the case of a nursing unit, the hours per unit of service is Worked Hours per Patient Day (HPPD).

Nursing department staffing grids may also display the resulting measures for Nurse-Patient Ratios or Direct Patient Care Hours per Patient Day. This is especially important if Nurse-Patient Ratios are subject to state or other mandates.

Looking at the highlighted row, at the budgeted census of 20, we see the following prescribed staffing:

SHIFT 1	SHIFT 2	SHIFT 3
1 - Manager (8 hr)		
4 - RN (12 hr)	4 - RN (12 hr)	
2 - LPN (*8 hr)	2 - LPN (8 hr)	2 - LPN (8 hr)
1 - Clerk (8 hr)	1 - Clerk (8 hr)	1 - Clerk (8 hr)

You may have noticed there are no RN's on Shift 3. Since they work 12-hour shifts, their 12-hour shifts are noted in Shift 1 and Shift 2.

MidWest Community Hospital

CC Number	6200
CC Name	3 South Med/Surg
Manager	Diane Snyder
Target	8.800 Worked Hours per Patient Day

Budget ADC	20
Max	32
Min	8

	Shift 1				Shift 2				Shift 3				Total Worked Hrs	HPPD
	Manager	RN	LPN	Clerk	Manager	RN	LPN	Clerk	Manager	RN	LPN	Clerk		
	8	12	8	8	8	12	8	8	8	12	8	8		
32	1	6	3	1		6	3	1			3	1	248	7.75
31	1	6	3	1		6	3	1			3	1	248	8.00
30	1	6	3	1		6	3	1			3	1	248	8.27
29	1	5	3	1		5	3	1			3	1	224	7.72
28	1	5	3	1		5	3	1			3	1	224	8.00
27	1	5	3	1		5	3	1			3	1	224	8.30
26	1	5	3	1		5	3	1			3	1	224	8.62
25	1	5	3	1		5	3	1			3	1	224	8.96
24	1	5	3	1		5	3	1			3	1	224	9.33
23	1	4	3	1		4	3	1			2	1	192	8.35
22	1	4	3	1		4	3	1			2	1	192	8.73
21	1	4	2	1		4	2	1			2	1	176	8.38
20	1	4	2	1		4	2	1			2	1	176	8.80
19	1	4	2	1		4	2	1			2	1	176	9.26
18	1	4	2	1		4	2	1			2	1	176	9.78
17	1	3	2	1		3	2	1			2	1	152	8.94
16	1	3	2	1		3	2	1			2	1	152	9.50
15	1	3	2	1		3	2	1			2	1	144	9.60
14	1	3	2	1		3	2	1			2	1	144	10.29
13	1	3	2	1		3	2	1			2	1	144	11.08
12	1	3	2	1		3	2	1			2	1	144	12.00
11	1	2	2	1		2	2	1			2	1	120	10.91
10	1	2	1	1		2	1	1			1	1	96	9.60
9	1	2	1	1		2	1	1			1	1	96	10.67
8	1	2	1	1		2	1	1			1	1	96	12.00

Exhibit 7.3

The chart in Exhibit 7.4, below, clearly shows the "modularity" of staffing. For example, at a census of 18, staffing at grid levels achieves a performance measure of 9.78 Worked Hours per Patient Day. At census levels of 19 through 21, staffing is held at the same levels and the resulting productivity measure improves to 9.26, 8.80 and, finally, 8.38. At a census of 22, the grid shows staffing adjustments that lead to a drop in performance — now 8.73.

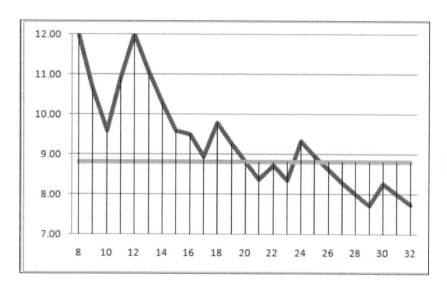

Exhibit 7.4

Nonetheless, when using the grid, the department manager approaches similar situations (patient service volumes) in a similar manner. When faced with an unusual situation, the manager may choose to "go off the grid" and staff as necessary to provide appropriate service levels. Remember, <u>the staffing grid serves as a guideline, not a mandate</u>. I recommend to managers that they keep notes on a daily printout, or interactive version, of the grid. This allows a director or, in the case of nursing departments the Chief Nursing Officer, to review staffing decisions and offer feedback or suggestions for future approaches.

An interactive grid could be a specific software product or even a spreadsheet and might look like the example below (see Exhibit 7.5). In the example below, staff enter patient census levels for each shift, review the grid-driven staffing suggestions, and then input actual staffing levels.

When the actual volume, in this case the midnight census, is entered the manager can review the approximate productivity performance for the day and for the period-to-date (fewer surprises from the productivity report!), as well as any notes posted by staff or shift supervisors. *See Exhibit 7.6 for an example of a period-to-date report.*

MidWest Community Hospital

Pay Period	25	
CC Number	6200	3 South Med/Surg
Target	8.800	Worked Hours per Patient Day

Date **Sunday, December 07, 2008**

Census

Shift 1	23
Shift 2	22
Shift 3	21
Midnight	21

Staffing

		Grid	Act
Shift 1			
Manager	8	1	0
RN	12	4	4
LPN	8	3	3
Clerk	8	1	1
Shift 2			
RN	12	4	4
LPN	8	3	3
Clerk	8	1	1
Shift 3			
LPN	8	2	2
Clerk	8	1	1

HPPD

Estimated	8.36
Actual	8.76

Exhibit 7.5

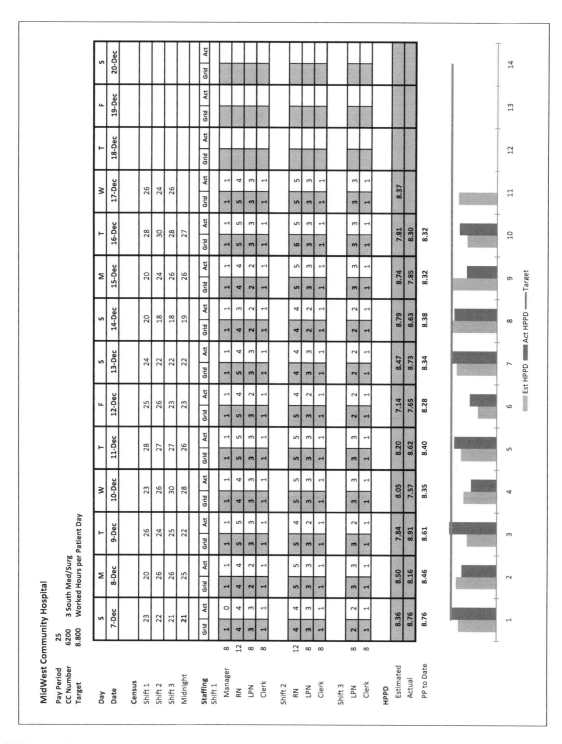

Exhibit 7.6

As noted earlier, while staffing grids are a tool generally associated with inpatient nursing units, they are also quite useful for managers of any variable departments with shifting client demands.

In the exhibits, below, staffing grids have been prepared for a Physical Therapy department. Staffing levels are driven by expected volumes. In this case, the volumes are in chargeable 15-minute equivalent units of service.

MidWest Community Hospital

CC Number	7420										Budget ADV	240	
CC Name	Physical Therapy										Max	384	
Manager	Bonnie Williamson										Min	96	
Target	0.450	Worked Hours per 15-Minute Equiv											

	Shift 1				Shift 2				Shift 3				Total	
	Manager	PT	PTA	Clerk	Manager	PT	PTA	Clerk	Manager	PT	PTA	Clerk	Worked Hrs	HPUOS
	8	8	8	8	8	8	8	8	8	8	8	8		
384	1	5	3	2		5	3	2					168	0.44
372	1	5	3	2		5	3	2					168	0.45
360	1	5	3	2		5	3	2					168	0.47
348	1	5	3	2		5	3	2					168	0.48
336	1	5	2	2		5	2	2					152	0.45
324	1	5	2	2		5	2	2					152	0.47
312	1	5	2	2		5	2	2					152	0.49
300	1	5	2	2		5	2	2					152	0.51
288	1	4	2	1		4	2	1					120	0.42
276	1	4	2	1		4	2	1					120	0.43
264	1	4	2	1		4	2	1					120	0.45
252	1	3	2	1		3	2	1					104	0.41
240	1	3	2	1		3	2	1					104	0.43
228	1	3	2	1		3	2	1					104	0.46
216	1	3	2	1		3	2	1					104	0.48
204	1	3	2	1		3	2	1					104	0.51
192	1	2	2	1		3	2	1					96	0.50
180	1	2	2	1		3	2	1					96	0.53
168	1	2	2	1		3	2	1					96	0.57
156	1	2	2	1		3	2	1					96	0.62
144	1	2	2	1		3	2	1					96	0.67
132	1	2	1	1		2	1	1					72	0.55
120	1	2	1	1		2	1	1					72	0.60
108	1	2	1	1		2	1	1					72	0.67
96	1	2	1	1		2	1	1					72	0.75

Exhibit 7.7

The next exhibit offers another example of a manager's daily input of estimated and actual volumes and the staffing proposed by the grid as compared to actual volumes and actual staffing. You will note it is different from the example shown in Exhibit 7.5. Again, this daily grid can be maintained on pad and paper, electronic worksheet, etc.

The key is to use the grid consistently. Also, periodically review previous entries and reports to answer the questions; "What worked?," "What didn't work?," "How did we respond to volume demands to yield maximum efficiency and effectiveness?," "Did we staff differently than the grid recommended and, if so, why would we do this or not do this again?"

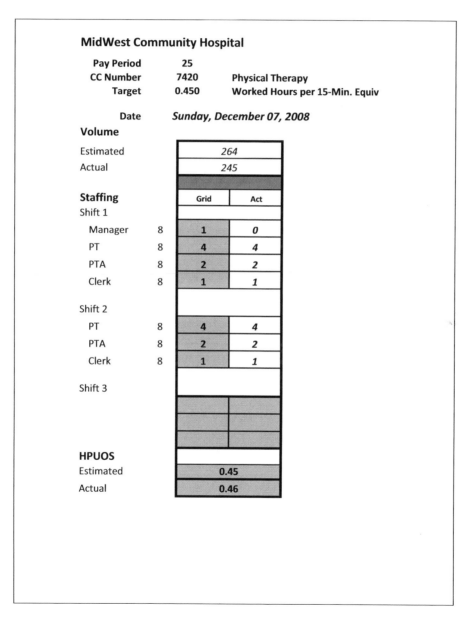

MidWest Community Hospital

Pay Period	25	
CC Number	7420	Physical Therapy
Target	0.450	Worked Hours per 15-Min. Equiv

Date	*Sunday, December 07, 2008*

Volume

Estimated		264
Actual		245

Staffing

		Grid	Act
Shift 1			
Manager	8	1	0
PT	8	4	4
PTA	8	2	2
Clerk	8	1	1
Shift 2			
PT	8	4	4
PTA	8	2	2
Clerk	8	1	1
Shift 3			

HPUOS

Estimated	0.45
Actual	0.46

Exhibit 7.8

Review:

1. Productivity reports are an obvious choice of tools for managing your departmental labor. But there are a number of other reports that you can use to verify the component data that is used to calculate your department's target and actual productivity.

2. The most helpful productivity reports enable a manager to quickly determine how well the department performed, identify possible trends and review supporting details.

3. Staffing Grids (or Staffing Matrices) are effective tools for staffing, relative to changing demand, in a consistent manner. If used correctly, these tools can be used both for real-time responsiveness as well as retrospective analysis of both what has worked and what has not.

EXERCISE 7.1 (Easy)

7.1.1 Referring to Exhibit 7.1: During which pay periods did the Physical Therapy department achieve Productivity Ratios greater than 90%?

7.1.2 Referring to Exhibit 7.1: In pay period ending April 6th, did the department perform at the 92nd percentile?

7.1.3 Referring to Exhibit 7.1: What was the average volume for the nine pay periods in the report?

7.1.4 Referring to Exhibit 7.1: What were the Target and Actual Worked Hours per Unit of Service for the pay period ending January 26th? How does the actual result compare with the average for the nine pay periods?

7.1.5 Referring to Exhibit 7.2: Has the Physical Therapy Department achieved its productivity targets during any of the pay periods in this report?

7.1.6 Referring to Exhibit 7.3: What are the total worked hours at each census level, from ADC = 18 to 21, if the department manager staffs according to the staffing grid? What are the Worked Hours per Patient Day measures for each of those census levels?

7.1.7 What does the graph in Exhibit 7.4 highlight?

EXERCISE 7.2   (Moderate)

7.2.1   Referring to Exhibit 7.1: This department has an overtime target of two to five percent. How has the department performed over the last nine periods? How has the department performed over the last four periods?

7.2.2   Referring to Exhibit 7.1: What is the annualized cost of the Physical Therapy department failing to achieve productivity targets for the nine pay periods to date?

7.2.3   Referring to Exhibit 7.1: On average, how many hours per pay period have been paid for overtime and contract labor? How many FTEs is this?

7.2.4   Referring to Exhibit 7.2: In which pay period did the department achieve the best efficiency measures? What's the simplest way to determine this?

7.2.5   Referring to Exhibit 7.3: At which census level will staffing according to the staffing grid provide the best productivity results? Which census levels are associated with the worst productivity measure?

7.2.6   Referring to Exhibit 7.3: What is the two word term used to describe the staffing levels at census = 10?

7.2.7   Referring to Exhibit 7.5: Looking at the manager's daily sheet, why is there a zero in the "Manager" box, instead of a one as prescribed by the staffing grid?

7.2.8 Referring to Exhibit 7.6: Looking at the manager's daily grid vs. actual report, how is the department performing for the period-to-date?

EXERCISE 7.3 (Challenging)

7.3.1 Referring to Exhibit 7.1: What would be the difference, in Paid FTEs, if the Physical Therapy department had achieved an average of 95% on their Productivity Ratios over the last nine pay periods?

7.3.2 Referring to Exhibit 7.1: If overtime hours were completely replaced by regular hours, what would be the annualized impact?

7.3.3 Referring to Exhibit 7.5: Looking at the manager's daily sheet, what accounts for the difference between the estimated and actual results?

7.3.4 Though the staffing grid is a planning tool, how can it also be effectively used for retrospective analysis?

Notes

Notes

Notes

....

....

....

....

....

....

....

....

8. Managing Productivity

Double-check Those Numbers!

Your department's actual labor productivity will be calculated based on productive hours and associated unit of service volumes. At the risk of repeating myself: one of the most basic tasks, in managing productivity, is to double-check the numbers upon which you will be judged!

Numerator - Productive Hours are generally the combination of Regular, Overtime, Education and Orientation payroll hours and Contract Labor hours. Be sure to review Time & Attendance reports regularly. I guarantee there will be errors! Likewise, review your periodic Accounting reports, showing contract labor hours and dollars attributed to your department (compare them to your own carefully kept notes).

Denominator — Make sure your department is getting credit for services provided. This is especially true in departments like Laboratory and Pharmacy where service charge items are being added, changed and deleted all of the time. Compare your productivity report volumes to the Revenue and Usage report, for the same period, to verify that volumes and, where appropriate, weightings have been correctly captured and applied.

Embrace the Volume!

The "Weakest Link" TV quiz show ran from April, 2001 to July 2002. Contestants could periodically choose to "bank their winnings" to protect them from loss due to incorrect answers. In variable demand departments, there are frequent opportunities for managers to bank their winnings. When faced with a surge in service demands, the manager can choose to ramp up staffing or, subject to any prescribed quality, regulatory and safety constraints, they can employ a measured, controlled response to that demand and bank the resulting improved productivity measures. I refer to this as "**embracing the volume**."

There will be countless other times when low volumes or unusual demands will result in poor productivity measures and savvy managers will be able to benefit from their "banked" positive productivity variances.

Staffing Mix — Full-time vs. Part-time

Whether you are the manager of a department with static volumes (such as Housekeeping or Maintenance) or dynamic volumes (Nursing, Ancillary, Dietary, etc.) a key method to maintain flexibility for staffing is to manage your department's mix of full-time and part-time staff. Recommendations run from 80/20 to 70/30 full-time to part-time FTEs, depending on the type of department. If all of a department's staff are full-time, then the only way to flex is to call them off or send them home. A number of nursing and ancillary department managers consider this their primary tool for flexing staffing levels. As I note below, staff become unhappy if given too many "unplanned PTO opportunities."

Managers, with part-time staff in their department, can better flex up and down as demand dictates. However, if a manager is working his part-time staff at full-time levels he may 1) lose the flexibility he requires, and 2) risk running afoul of labor regulations that might require converting staff to full-time employees.

Foundational Staffing

The "science" of Foundational Staffing is simply the discipline of identifying your department's "steady state" staffing requirements. Too many department managers staff their departments for the worst case scenario.

> I once met with the manager of a large hospital's Plant and Engineering department. We were reviewing each member of his department and their responsibilities. Two were engineers in the Cogeneration plant. I mentioned that, in my earlier walk-through, that area had seemed rather quiet. The manager acknowledged that, due to declining energy costs, the plant had been idled the prior year. When I inquired of the two engineers, he stated they were there "just in case" and were used elsewhere as needed. I then asked about one of the staff on the night shift. He replied the employee was there in case the water was shut off. In that event, someone had to make sure the re-start was successful, all toilets were running properly again, etc. I asked when the water was last shut off. It had been over two years. He agreed that, rather than staff for a worst case scenario, perhaps it would be best to pay the overtime for a rare "all hands on deck" call-back.

Yes, this is an extreme example but, after years of conversations with managers, I find many are staffing for the worst case scenario to some degree. Rather than staff for the exception, managers should identify their "foundational demand", staff accordingly and flex up using overtime, per diem pool, or contract labor to address unusual surges in demand (and staff down as needed).

The following exhibits offer an example of assessing your foundational staffing level. In Exhibit 8.1, below, we see department Volumes compared to Productive and Paid FTEs.

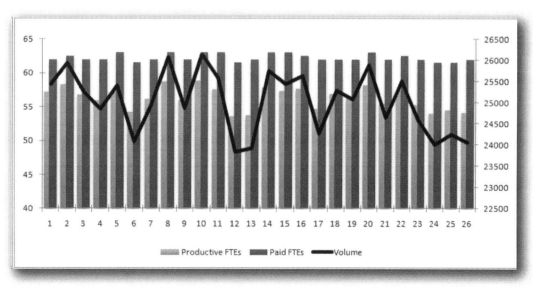

Exhibit 8.1

In Exhibit 8.2, Paid FTEs are removed, to see the correlation between Volumes and Productive (Worked) FTEs. There is a strong correlation. We can see variation above and below the dotted Average Productive FTEs line. This manager is clearly managing her productive staff relative to changing demands.

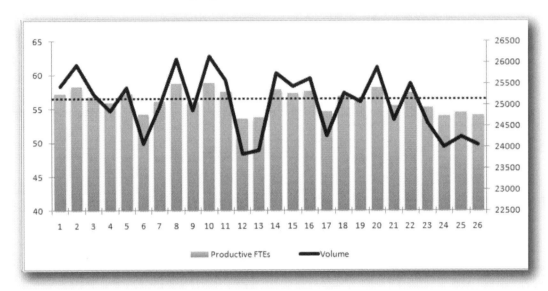

Exhibit 8.2

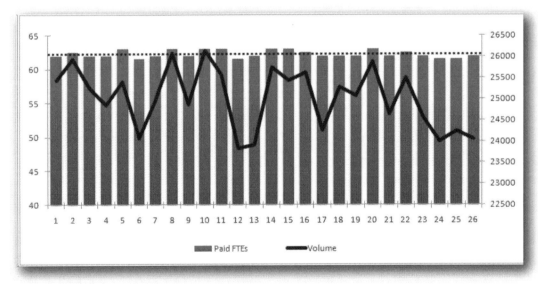

Exhibit 8.3

However, in Exhibit 8.3, we see a troubling trend. This exhibit compares Volumes to Paid FTEs — there is no correlation. There is little variation above and below the dotted Average Paid FTEs line. This manager is using only one of the tools at her disposal — flexing down. She staffs for the highest demand levels and calls off and/or sends home staff when the demand volumes don't materialize.

Yes, this manager does manage her department's labor productivity. But, just as when you paddle a canoe only on one side, her progress may be short-lived. In the many years I have asked department managers to indicate if their employees really like all those "unplanned vacations" only one has ever raised her hand...

The science of assessing your foundational demand is in reviewing historical levels of demand as well as efficient and effective staffing at those levels. Those staffing grids, with annotations, will come in very handy here!

1. **Identify general demand levels.**

    a. What has cause demand spikes in the past? Are they cyclical? Can they be forecasted?

    b. Are there any planned or budgeted changes to your services? Can you put a number on the impact to your department's services and on your staff?

2. **Identify staffing mix and levels required to support foundational demand.**

    a. Do you have the mix of full-time and part-time staff necessary to allow you to flex staffing to demand?

    b. Do you have administrative approval to utilize overtime to address demand surges?

    c. Do you have an in-house per diem or float pool from which you can draw qualified resources?

    d. Do you have approval to draw resources from contract labor or agency staffing when needed?

    e. Staffing in this manner, will you be able to achieve budgeted productivity targets?

3. Identify the staff surplus to your department's foundational requirements.

    a. Can these staff be assigned to other, understaffed departments?

    b. Can they be cross-trained to support other departments?

When Administrative approvals are secured and plans for change are in drafted, select representatives who are "Champions of Change" to review the draft. Discuss the logic for this approach and how it can be in the best interests of the department, and the hospital, to enact them. Show them, with glance-able, understandable displays, how the demand and associated staffing were determined. Solicit their feedback on changes to the plan to better ensure it's success and to make their department a best-performing department — in both efficiency and effectiveness!!

Overtime and Contract Labor

Overtime and contract (agency) staffing, when used appropriately, can be an effective mechanism for responding to surges in demand. This assumes the department managers have systems in place for consistent, appropriate staffing to foundational demands.

In many hospitals, Senior Management has taken up the banner of:

NO CONTRACT LABOR!

I've worked with a hospital wherein the Administrator proudly proclaimed that he had made progress toward eliminating all contract labor utilization — by <u>hiring</u> all of the Traveler staff. Unfortunately, this had been done without first assessing the underlying productivity of any of the departments!

In the last twenty years, I have worked with many "desperately ill" hospitals. Almost without exception, when I asked the Chief Nursing Officer what the Agency and Traveler costs were running, the answer was, "I don't know."

I have painted an alternative to the aforementioned banner. Rather than "NO Contract Labor!", my banner reads:

KNOW CONTRACT LABOR!

It is critical to <u>manage</u> your contract labor. Keep a careful eye on utilization of contracted staff. Utilization of Travelers should be kept to a minimum as you are locked into a defined term of employment.

Likewise, overtime hours should be carefully managed and, if necessary, require administrative approval. In the guise of staffing to foundational levels, a case can be made for variable demand departments to utilize this tool. For support and administrative departments, with relatively level demand volumes, overtime utilization should be an exception.

Ask the "Dumb" Questions!

The story goes: Karolyn, a young newlywed, wants to prepare her first Christmas ham, so she calls her mother for the recipe. Mom gives her instructions for preparing the traditional glaze, cooking container and time and reminds her "Don't forget to trim off both ends before glazing and putting it in the oven!" Puzzled, our heroine inquires "Why?" "I don't know, I just learned it that way from MY mom!" replies her mother. Next, Karolyn, calls her grandmother and asks about the requisite trimming. "Well, that's the way my Aunt Gertrude used to do it, and I always loved her Christmas ham!", replied Grandma. Finally, Karolyn phones Great Aunt Gertrude, in Shady Acres Assisted Living, about the ham recipe. "Why did I slice off the ends?", replied Great Aunt Gertrude. "That's easy! I sliced off the ends because our oven was too small !!"

Admit it: the story is not that far off from some of our longstanding departmental processes.

Sometimes it's important to keep pressing ahead, asking the "Dumb Questions." I call it the discipline of the "SEVEN WHYs." Examples include:

"<u>Why</u> do we approach it that way?"

"<u>Why</u> do we make those additional copies if we never use them?"

<u>Why</u> do we perform this task manually when there are machines that will perform it with higher quality and more efficiently?

"<u>Why</u> doesn't this department's staffing pattern correlate to our demand patterns?"

<u>Why</u> do we perform these tasks or steps at all, when they don't add any value to the services we provide? Do our customers value these tasks?

"<u>Why</u> does this department perform this task if its also provided by another department?

"<u>Why</u> have we taken on this additional service?"
"Is it consistent with our hospital's strategy and mission?"

"<u>Why</u> do we deliver that service at all?"

Try it even with some of your most time venerated processes and services. Your effort will not lack for eyebrow-raising answers...

Review:

1. Reviewing the accuracy of department hours — payroll and contract labor — as well as volumes are key responsibilities for department managers who want to take control of their departments' labor productivity management.

2. When faced with a surge in service demands, a manager can choose to simply add staff or, assuming requisite quality of service is maintained, employ a measured, controlled response to that demand and "bank" the resulting improved productivity measures.

3. Having an available complement of part-time staff, to flex in response to changing service demands, is another labor productivity management best-practice.

4. The science of Foundational Staffing is simply the discipline of identifying your department's steady state staffing requirements. Too many department managers staff their departments for the worst case scenario.

5. Overtime, float pool and contract labor staffing, when managed closely, can be effective mechanisms for responding to surges in service demand. This assumes that department managers have systems in place for consistent, appropriate staffing to foundational demands.

Notes

Notes

Notes

9. Solutions to Exercises

EXERCISE 3.1   (Easy)

3.1.1   Labor Productivity is measured in:

    a.   Total Paid FTEs as a percent of Budgeted FTEs.

    b.   Staff per Facility Patient Day.

    c.   Productive hours per Unit of Service.

    d.   None of the above.

    Answer: c. Labor Productivity is generally measured in Productive (Worked) Hours per Unit of Service.

3.1.2   Productive Hours, also often referred to as Worked Hours, are typically a combination of:

    a.   Regular Hours, Overtime Hours and On-call Hours

    b.   Regular Hours, Overtime Hours, On-call Hours and Contract Labor hours

    c.   Regular Hours, Overtime Hours, Contract Labor Hours and Education/Orientation hours.

    d.   Regular Hours and Contract Labor hours.

    Answer: c. Productive Hours, also often referred to as "Worked Hours", are a combination of Regular Hours, Overtime Hours, Contract Labor Hours and Education/Orientation hours.

3.1.3   A department's productivity report shows 3,460 worked hours in the most recent pay period. How many Worked FTEs ("Productive FTEs") is this?

    Answer: 3,460 Worked Hours / 80 Hours per FTE per Pay Period = **43.3 Worked FTEs**

3.1.4   The Laboratory department has a productivity target of 0.175 Worked Hours per Billed Test. Calculate the department's Target Worked Hours for a pay period when the volume was 20,000 Billed Tests.

Answer: 20,000 Billed Tests x 0.175 Worked Hours per Billed Test = **3,500 Worked Hours**

3.1.5   Referring to the information in 3.1.4: The department's actual Worked Hours totaled 3,360. What was the actual Worked Hours per Billed Test for the period?

Answer: 3,360 Worked Hours / 20,000 Billed Tests = **0.168 Worked Hours per Billed Test**

3.1.6   What is the ADC for a nursing unit with 316 Patient Days in a pay period?

Answer: 316 Patient Days / 14 Days = **22.6 Average Daily Census (ADC)**

3.1.7   Department 6023 had a volume of 11,315 Patient Days in the previous year. In the same period, staff worked 105,230 hours (productive time). What were the Total Hours per Patient Day (HPPD) for the period?

Answer: 105,230 Worked Hours / 11,315 Patient Days = **9.30 Worked Hours per Patient Day**

3.1.8   Department 6024 had 273 Patient Days in the most recent pay period. If their productivity target (staffing standard) is 7.76 Worked Hours per Patient Day (HPPD), how many Target Worked FTEs do they have for the period?

Answer: 273 Patient Days x 7.76 Worked Hours per Patient Day =

2,119 Target Worked Hours

2,119 Worked Hours / 80 Hours per Pay Period =

26.5 Worked FTEs

EXERCISE 3.2 (Moderate)

3.2.1 Equivalent Patient Days are:

    a. The combination of a nursing unit's patient days and admissions.

    b. Designed to give nursing units some credit for observation activity

    c. The combination of a nursing unit's patient days and observation hours/24

    d. All of the above.

    e. b and c.

Answer: e. Equivalent Patient Days are designed to give nursing units some credit for observation activity. They are calculated by adding Patient Days and (Observation Hours/24) for the review period.

3.2.2 Adjusted Patient Days and Adjusted Discharges are:

    a. Generally used as a denominator, reflecting a hospital's scale of services. Hospital-wide or support departments' FTEs then divided by Adjusted Patient Days or Adjusted Discharges, to show their size in relationship to the scale of services supported.

    b. Hospital Total Inpatient Adult and Pediatric Days, or Discharges, multiplied by an "Adjustment Factor" that gives credit for demands associated with outpatient activity.

    c. a and b.

    d. none of the above.

Answer: c. Hospital Total Inpatient Adult and Pediatric Days, or Discharges are multiplied by an "Adjustment Factor" that gives credit for outpatient activity. The Adjusted Patient Days and Adjusted Discharges are generally used as a denominator, reflecting a hospital's scale of services. Hospital-wide or support departments' FTEs are then divided by the Adjusted Patient Days or Adjusted

Discharges for the period, to show their size relative to the scale of services supported.

3.2.3   Using the data provided in 3.1.3, Non-Productive Hours were 12% of Productive hours for the pay period. What was the department's Total Paid Hours for that pay period?

Answer: 3,460 Worked Hours x 1.12 Paid:Productive Ratio = **3,875.2 Paid Hours**

3.2.4   Using the results from 3.2.3, What was the department's total Paid FTEs?

Answer: 3,875.2 Paid Hours / 80 Hours per FTE per Pay Period = **48.4 Paid FTEs**

EXERCISE 3.3   (Challenging)

3.3.1   An ICU has a Core Staffing level of two nurses around the clock.
How many Worked (Productive) FTEs does that equate to?

Answer: 2 RNs x 24 Hours per Day x 365 Days per Year / 2080 Hours per FTE per Year = **8.4 Worked FTEs**

3.3.2   MidWest Community Hospital's Outpatient Physical Therapy Department has the schedule, below, for the next pay period:

Monday — Friday
        1 - Manager (8 hrs/day)
        4 - Physical Therapists (8 hrs/day)
        2 - Physical Therapy Assistants (8 hrs/day)
        1 - Clerk (8 hrs/day)

Saturday
        2 - Physical Therapists (8 hrs/day)
        1 - Clerk (8 hrs/day)

Sunday (closed)

How many Worked FTEs have been scheduled for the pay period?

Answer:

Monday — Friday
1 - Manager	1 Staff x 8 Hrs/Day x 5 Days/Wk x 2 Wks/PP = 80 Hours
4 - Phys. Therapists	4 Staff x 8 Hrs/Day x 5 Days/Wk x 2 Wks/PP = 320 Hours
2 - PTAs	2 Staff x 8 Hrs/Day x 5 Days/Wk x 2 Wks/PP = 160 Hours
1 - Clerk	1 Staff x 8 Hrs/Day x 5 Days/Wk x 2 Wks/PP = 80 Hours

Saturday
2 - Phys. Therapists	2 Staff x 8 Hrs/Day x 1 Day/Wk x 2 Wks/PP = 32 Hours
1 - Clerk (8 hrs/day)	1 Staff x 8 Hrs/Day x 1 Day/Wk x 2 Wks/PP = 16 Hours

Total Hours Worked/PP = 80+320+160+80+32+16 = 688 Worked Hours

688 Worked Hours / 80 Hours per Pay Period = **8.6 Worked FTEs**

Answer Shortcut 1:

Monday — Friday: 8 staff x 8 Hrs/Day x 5 Days per Wk x 2 Wks per PP =
640 Worked Hours

Saturday: 3 staff x 8 Hrs/Day x 1 Day per Wk x 2 Wks per PP =
48 Worked Hours

Total = 640 Worked Hours + 48 Worked Hours = 688 Worked Hours

688 Worked Hours /80 Hours per Pay Period = **8.6 Worked FTEs**

Answer Shortcut 2:

8 staff work 40-hr weeks = 8 FTEs.

3 staff work 48 hours per pay period (48/80=0.6 FTEs)

Combined total = **8.6 Worked FTEs**

3.3.3   MidWest Community Hospital had 120,450 Adjusted Patient Days, and 1,617 Paid FTEs this past year. What was their Paid FTEs per AOB?

Answer: 120,450 Adjusted Patient Days / 365 Days per Year =
330 Adjusted Occupied Beds (AOBs)
1,617 FTEs / 330 AOB = **4.9 Paid FTEs per AOB**

3.3.4   Using the results from 3.1.4, if Non-Productive Hours equal 9% of Productive, for the reviewed period, what was the Total Target Paid Hours for that period?

Answer: 3,500 Target Worked Hours x 1.09 Paid:Productive Ratio =
3,815 Target Paid Hours

3.3.5   Using the results from 3.3.4, how many Paid FTEs does that equate to?

Answer: 3,815 Paid Hours / 80 Hours per FTE per Pay Period =
47.7 Paid FTEs

3.3.6   The 3 East Medical Unit recorded 744 Patient Days and 2,604 Observation Hours for the month of December. What was their Equivalent Patient Days total for the month?

Answer: 2,604 Observation Hours / 24 Observation Hours per EPD = 108.5 Equivalent Patient Days (EPDs)
744 Patient Days + 108.5 EPDs = **852.5 Equivalent Patient Days**

3.3.7   The OB/Gyn Unit recorded 224 Patient Days and 336 Observation Hours for the month of February. What was their Equivalent Patient Days total for the month?

Answer: 336 Observation Hours / 24 Observation Hours per EPD = 14 Equivalent Patient Days
224 Patient Days + 14 Equivalent Patient Days = **238 Equivalent Patient Days**

3.3.8   MidWest Community Hospital shows $814 million in Total Charges (Gross Patient Revenues) for the year. Of that, $472 million is Inpatient Charges. What is the resulting Adjustment Factor?

Answer: $814M Gross Patient Revs / $472M Gross Inpatient Revs = **1.725**

3.3.9   Using the Adjustment Factor in 3.3.8, and the Adjusted Patient Days in 3.3.3, what was the Average Daily Census for the hospital that year?
[please round to the nearest Day]

Answer: 120,450 Adjusted Patient Days / 1.725 Adjustment Factor = 69,826 Patient Days
69,826 Patient Days / 365 Days per Year = **191 Average Daily Census**

3.3.10 Referring to 3.3.3: If the hospital's global staffing target is 4.75 Paid FTEs per AOB, how many FTEs are they away from their target?
[please round to the nearest FTE]

Answer: Question 3.3.3 showed 330 Adj. Occupied Beds (AOBs) and 4.9 Paid FTEs per AOB for the year.

Target - Actual Paid FTEs per AOB = 4.90 - 4.75 FTEs per AOB = 0.15 Paid FTEs/AOB.
0.15 Paid FTEs per AOB x 330 AOBs = **50 Paid FTEs**

EXERCISE 4.1   (Easy)

Fred Bachofen is the manager of MidWest Community Hospital's Laboratory
Department. For the most recent two-week pay period, his productivity report shows:

Department Volume	25,000 Billed Tests
Regular Hours	3,995
Overtime Hours	243
Non-Productive Hours	470
Staffing Standard (Target)	0.165 Worked Hours per Billed Test

4.1.1   What was Fred's department's average daily volume of Billed Tests?

Answer: 25,000 Billed Tests / 14 Days per Pay Period = **1,786 per Day**

4.1.2   How many Productive Hours did department staff work this pay period?

Answer: 3,995 Regular Hours + 243 Overtime Hours =
4,238 Productive (Worked) Hours

4.1.3   How many Paid Hours did department staff work this pay period?

Answer: 4,238 Productive Hours + 470 Non-Productive Hours =
4,708 Paid Hours

4.1.4   How many Productive FTEs worked this pay period?

Answer: 4,238 Productive Hours / 80 Hours per Pay Period =
53.0 Productive (Worked) FTEs

4.1.5   How many Paid FTEs did Fred's department have this period?

Answer: 4,708 Paid Hours / 80 Hours per Pay Period = **58.9 Paid FTEs**

EXERCISE 4.2   (Moderate)

Using the data provided in Exercise 4.1:

4.2.1   What was the total Target Productive Hours for the most recent pay period?

Answer: 25,000 Billed Tests x 0.165 Worked Hours per Billed Test =
4,125 Productive (Worked) Hours

4.2.2   What was the Actual Worked Hours per UOS for the pay period?

Answer: 4,238 Worked Hours / 25,000 Billed Tests =
0.170 Worked Hours per Billed Test

4.2.3   Was Fred's department's performance better or worse than target?

Answer: 0.170 Actual Worked Hours per UOS > 0.165 Target Worked Hours
per UOS = **Worse**

4.2.4   What was the resulting Productivity Ratio for the pay period?

Answer: 4,125 Target Worked Hours / 4,238 Actual Worked Hours = 0.97 = **97%**

EXERCISE 4.3   (Challenging)

Using the data provided in Exercise 4.1:

4.3.1   Given the same volume, how many fewer hours would Fred's staff have to work to achieve the Target Worked Hours per Billed Test?

Answer: 4,238 Actual Worked Hours - 4,125 Target Worked Hours = **113 Worked Hours**

4.3.2   How many billed tests would Fred's staff need to perform, with no additional hours, to achieve their productivity target?

Answer: 4,238 Actual Worked Hours / 0.165 Target Worked Hours per Billed Test = **25,685 Billed Tests**

4.3.3   What was the department's Non-Productive Hours as a Percent of Total Productive Hours for the period?

Answer: 470 Non-Productive Hours / 4,238 Productive Hours = **11.1%**

4.3.4   What was the department's Non-Productive Hours as a Percent of Total Paid Hours for the period?

Answer: 470 Non-Productive Hours / 4,708 Paid Hours = **10.0%**

EXERCISE 4.4   (Easy)

Sylvia Weber is the manager of 3 South — one of MidWest Community Hospital's Medical Surgical Units. For the most recent two-week pay period, her report shows:

Department Volume 1	385 Patient Days
Department Volume 2	252 Observation Hours
Regular Hours	3,244
Overtime Hours	198
Education/Orientation Hours	42
Non-Productive Hours	561
Staffing Standard (Target)	8.3 Worked Hours per Equiv. Patient Day

Note: All hours include all department staff.

4.4.1   What was the ADC for the unit for this pay period?

Answer: 385 Patient Days / 14 Days per Pay Period =
27.5 Average Daily Census (ADC)

4.4.2   Please convert the Observation Hours to Equivalent Patient Days (EPD).

Answer: 252 Observation Hours / 24 Observation Hours per EPD =
10.5 Equivalent Patient Days

4.4.3   How many Total Equivalent Patient Days did 3 South staff support?

Answer: 385 Patient Days + 10.5 Equivalent Patient Days =
395.5 Total Equivalent Patient Days

4.4.4 Excluding Overtime Hours, what was the Actual Worked Hours per Equivalent Patient Day?

Answer: 3,244 Regular Hours + 42 Education/Orientation Hours = 3,286 Worked Hours

3,286 Worked Hours / 395.5 Equivalent Patient Days = **8.3 Worked Hours per Equivalent Patient Day**.

4.4.5 What was the Total Worked Hours per Equivalent Patient Day?

Answer: 3,244 Regular Hours + 198 Overtime Hours + 42 Education/Orientation Hours = 3,484 Worked Hours

3,484 Worked Hours / 395.5 Equivalent Patient Days = **8.8 Worked Hours per EPD**.

4.4.6 How many Productive FTEs worked this pay period?

Answer: 3,484 Total Worked Hours / 80 Hours per FTE per Pay Period = **43.6 Productive (Worked) FTEs**

4.4.7 How many Paid FTEs did Sylvia's department have this period?

Answer: 3,484 Total Worked (Productive) Hours + 561 Non-Productive Hours = 4,045 Total Paid Hours

4,045 Paid Hours / 80 Hours per FTE per Pay Period = **50.6 Paid FTEs**

EXERCISE 4.5   **(Moderate)**

Using the data provided in Exercise 4.4:

4.5.1   What was the Target Productive Hours for the most recent pay period?

   Answer: 395.5 Equivalent Patient Days x 8.3 Worked Hours per Patient Day = **3,283 Productive (Worked) Hours**

4.5.2   Was 3 South's performance better or worse than target?

   Answer: 3,484 Actual Worked Hours > 3,283 Target Worked Hours = **Worse**

4.5.3   What is the resulting Productivity Ratio for the pay period?

   Answer: 3,283 Target Worked Hours / 3,484 Actual Worked Hours = 0.94 = **94%**

EXERCISE 4.6   (Challenging)

Using the data provided in Exercise 4.4:

4.6.1   Approximately how many FTEs of overtime did Sylvia utilize during
        the pay period?

   Answer: 198 Overtime Hours / 80 Hours per FTE per Pay Period = **2.5 FTEs**

4.6.2   What was the department's Non-Productive Hours as a Percent of Total
        Productive Hours for the period?   [Budget Focus]

   Answer: 561 Non-Productive Hours / 3,484 Productive (Worked) Hours = **16.1%**

4.6.3   What was the department's Non-Productive Hours as a Percent of Total Paid
        Hours for the period?

   Answer: 561 Non-Productive Hours / 4,045 Paid Hours = **13.9%**

EXERCISE 4.7 (Easy)

4.7.1 MidWest Community Hospital has contracted with a national firm to provide management for their Food and Nutrition department. True or False: these 3.0 FTEs are no longer included in the department's productivity report.

Answer: False. The outsourced management hours are to be included in department actual hours just as agency or other contract labor is included.

4.7.2 A hospital's Accounting department has a Fixed staffing target of 8.5 Paid FTEs. The most recent productivity report shows department staffing at 9.0 FTEs - down from 9.3 FTEs the prior year.

a. As the department is "Fixed", their actual productivity does not matter.

b. The department was staffed at 9.3 FTEs, last year, so they have improved. The current Fixed Target is not a troubling issue.

c. The department has a 0.5 Paid FTE unfavorable variance.

d. The department manager should assess department volume demands and revisit benchmarked staffing levels to see if there is justification for a periodic adjustment of the Fixed Target.

e. c and d

Answer: e. While the department has seen a reduction of staffing, from 9.3 to 9.0 Paid FTEs, they are still not achieving the target of 8.5 Paid FTEs. It is, however, appropriate to review Fixed Departments to see if demand volumes have risen or fallen, to see if the current fixed targets are still appropriate.

Reviews of fixed department targets should be conducted quarterly or semi-annually, to see if supported volumes have increased or decreased and to determine if current staffing targets are appropriate in light of current and forecasted patient service support requirements.

4.7.3   True/False: Departments with multiple staffing standards, or Fixed & Variable staffing standards, will see their summarized target (Worked Hours per Summary Unit of Service) change from period to period.

Answer: True. From one period to the next, the department's mix will change, whether the mix of services or mix of variable vs. fixed, yielding a change in the resulting summarized Worked Hours per UOS measure.

The staffing standards themselves have not changed, just the mix of services or the fixed and variable proportions.

EXERCISE 4.8   (Moderate)

4.8.1   Which of the following units of service is <u>not</u> considered "static"?

    a. Square Feet Cleaned

    b. Devices Maintained

    c. Surgery Minutes

    d. Employees

    Answer: c. Surgery Minutes is a "dynamic" unit of service measure. The volume is subject to change, from period to period, and is cumulative for each day in that period.

4.8.2   True/False: Departments with static staffing standards should not be included in hospital productivity reports.

    Answer: False. Even though their staffing targets may remain largely un-changed, from one period to the next, managers of departments with static staffing standards are still accountable for achieving those targets each period.

4.8.3   A rural hospital provides both urgent and emergency care services in their Emergency Department. The department has separate staffing standards for each level of service: 2.50 Worked Hours per Emergency Visit and 1.20 Worked Hours per Urgent Care visit. The department's Summary Unit of Service is "Total Visits".

    Department statistics for the most recent pay period show 562 Emergency Visits and 459 Urgent Care Visits. What was the department's overall Worked Hours per Visit target for the period?

Answer: 562 Emergency Visits x 2.50 Worked Hours per Visit = 1,405 Target Worked Hours

459 Urgent Care Visits x 1.20 Worked Hours per Visit = 551 Target Worked Hours

1,405 + 551 = 1,956 Total Target Worked Hours

562 Emergency Visits + 459 Urgent Care Visits = 1,021 Total Visits

1,956 Total Hours / 1,021 Total Visits = **1.92 Worked Hours per Visit**

4.8.4   Using the staffing standards in 4.8.3, if department statistics for the prior pay period showed 522 Emergency Visits and 399 Urgent Care Visits, what was the department's overall Target Worked Hours per Visit for the period?

Answer: 522 Emergency Visits x 2.50 Worked Hours per Visit = 1,305 Target Worked Hours

399 Urgent Care Visits x 1.20 Worked Hours per Visit = 479 Target Worked Hours

1,305 + 479 = 1,784 Total Target Worked Hours

522 Emergency Visits + 399 Urgent Care Visits = 921 Total Visits

1,784 Total Hours / 921 Total Visits = **1.94 Worked Hours per Visit**

4.8.5   Referring to 4.8.3 and 4.8.4, why did the Worked Hours per Visit target change from one pay period to the next?

Answer: The mix of services changed. Note how the staffing standards used for Emergency Visits versus Urgent Visits did not change. Emergency Visits were a larger proportion of Total Visits in the prior pay period, so the overall Worked Hours per Visit measure decreased from 1.94 to 1.92.

EXERCISE 4.9 (Challenging)

4.9.1 MidWest Community Hospital's Laundry department processes approximately 2.2 million pounds of laundry per year. The department's productivity target is 1.45 Worked Hours per 100 pounds processed.

If the volume for the most recent month was 195,000 pounds, what was the department's Worked FTEs target?

Answer: 195,000 lbs processed / 100 = 1,950 100-lbs processed

1.45 Worked Hours per 100-lbs processed x 1,950 100-lbs processed = 2,828 Worked Hours

2,828 Worked Hours / 173.33 Hours per FTE per month = **16.3 Worked FTEs**

4.9.2 Community Hospital of Sulphur Glen is building a replacement hospital facility. At 168,000 square feet, it is considerably larger than the old facility (129,000 sq ft). Mark Arnold, the Plant/Maintenance Manager, is preparing a budget for staffing the new facility. His current position control report shows 3.0 FTEs.

Mark's goal is to staff the department at the top quartile benchmark of 50.0 Worked Hours per Thousand Square Feet Maintained (annual). If the Paid-to-Productive ratio has been 1.12 for the past twelve months, approximately how many additional Paid FTEs will Mark request?

Answer: 168,000 Sq Ft Maintained / 1,000 = 168 1,000-Sq Ft Maintained

50.0 Worked Hours per 1,000-Sq Ft Maintained x 168 1,000-Sq Ft Maintained = 8,400 Worked Hours

8,400 Worked Hours x 1.12 Paid-to-Productive = 9,408 Paid Hours

9,408 Paid Hours / 2080 Hours per FTE per year = 4.5 Paid FTEs

Mark will likely request 4.5 Paid FTEs - an increase of 1.5 FTEs.

4.9.3   Painted Hills Memorial Hospital employs a combined Fixed/Variable productivity staffing standard. The Food and Nutrition department's productivity target includes 2.0 Fixed Paid FTEs, for the manager and one assistant. The department's variable target is 0.15 Worked Hours per Meal Equivalent (a unit of service that combines patient meals with equivalents calculated from cafeteria sales, nutritional supplements, etc.).

The department's Meal Equivalent volume totaled 11,814 in the most recent pay period. If the Paid-to-Productive ratio for the period was 1.09, what was the resulting Total Paid Hours target? How many Paid FTEs is that?

Answer: 0.15 Worked Hours per Meal Equivalent x 11,814 Meal Equivalents = 1,772 Worked Hours

1,772 Worked Hours x 1.09 Paid-to-Productive = 1,932 Paid Hours

2 Paid FTEs x 80 Hours per FTE = 160 Paid Hours

1,932 Paid Hours + 160 Paid Hours = **2,092 Total Paid Hours**

2,092 Paid Hours / 80 Hours per FTE per Pay Period = **26.2 Paid FTEs**

EXERCISE 7.1   (Easy)

7.1.1   Referring to Exhibit 7.1: During which pay periods did the Physical Therapy department achieve Productivity Ratios greater than 90%?

Answer: Pay periods ending 2/9 (94%), 3/9 (91%) and 4/6 (92%).

7.1.2   Referring to Exhibit 7.1: In the pay period ending April 6th, did the department perform at the 92nd percentile?

Answer: No. The department performed at 92% of the productivity target, as measured by the formula: Target Worked Hours / Actual Worked Hours.

7.1.3   Referring to Exhibit 7.1: What was the average volume for the nine pay periods in the report?

Answer: 1,581 Timed Treatments, as displayed in the column titled "RPT AVG".

7.1.4   Referring to Exhibit 7.1: What were the Target and Actual Worked Hours per Unit of Service for the pay period ending January 26th? How does the actual result compare with the average for the nine pay periods?

Answer: Target Worked Hours per UOS was 0.45, Actual was 0.55. Worse - Actual Worked Hours per UOS for the nine periods averaged 0.51, nine percent better than the results for PPE January 26.

7.1.5   Referring to Exhibit 7.2: Has the Physical Therapy Department achieved its productivity targets during any of the pay periods in this report?

Answer: No. Actual Worked Hours have been greater than Target for each of the nine pay periods.

7.1.6　Referring to Exhibit 7.3: If the department manager staffs according to the staffing grid, what Total Worked hours should result at each census level from ADC = 18 to 21? What are the Worked Hours per Patient Day measures for each of those census levels?

Answer: 176 worked hours. 18 = 9.78, 19 = 9.26, 20 = 8.80 and 21 = 8.38 worked hours per patient day

7.1.7　What does the graph in Exhibit 7.4 highlight?

Answer: Staffing is modular not linear or "the modularity of staffing."

EXERCISE 7.2   (Moderate)

7.2.1   Referring to Exhibit 7.1: This department has an overtime target of two to five percent. How has the department performed over the last nine periods? How has the department performed over the last four periods?

Answer: For the nine pay periods in the report, the department performed at 5.3% - slightly worse than target. Of the four most recent pay periods, only one pay period's result was within the target range. In fact, pay period ending 03/23 was at 7.7%.

7.2.2   Referring to Exhibit 7.1: What is the annualized cost of the Physical Therapy department failing to achieve productivity targets for the nine pay periods to date?

Answer: The average cost of missing productivity targets over the past nine pay periods = $2,284 (see "RPT AVG" column for "$ Impact Prod" row).

$2,284 per pay period x 26 pay periods per year = **$59,384 per year.**

7.2.3   Referring to Exhibit 7.1: On average, how many hours per pay period have been paid for overtime and contract labor? How many FTEs is this?

Answer: The average overtime hours for the nine pay periods = 43

Average contract labor hours for the nine pay periods = 37

Average overtime and contract labor hours = 43 + 37 = **80**

80 hours / 80 hours per pay period = **1.0 FTE**

7.2.4   Referring to Exhibit 7.2: In which pay period did the department achieve the best efficiency measures? What's the simplest way to determine this?

Answer: Pay Period Ending Feb 9. There's several ways to quickly determine this: The summary boxes at the bottom of the page (color coded green/yellow/red) and the graph showing Productivity Ratios. Also, the Productivity Ratios are displayed at the top of Exhibit 7.1 (but this question is about Exhibit 7.2).

7.2.5   Referring to Exhibit 7.3: At which census level will staffing according to the staffing grid provide the best productivity results? Which census levels are associated with the worst productivity measure?

Answer: Census = 29. Census = 8 and Census = 12.

7.2.6   Referring to Exhibit 7.3: What is the two word term used to describe the staffing levels at census = 10?

Answer: Core Staffing Level (or Minimum Staffing).

7.2.7   Referring to Exhibit 7.5: Looking at the manager's daily sheet, why is there a zero in the "Manager" box, instead of a one as prescribed by the staffing grid?

Answer: It's a Sunday. The manager is designated on the grid as an 8-hour, Shift 1 position. This grid does not differentiate weekdays from weekends (though some do). Important: In this grid, the manager, though an RN, is not factored into Nurse:Patient ratios.

7.2.8   Referring to Exhibit 7.6: Looking at the manager's daily grid vs. actual report, how is the department performing for the period-to-date?

Answer: Favorably. The period-to-date actual result is 8.32 Worked Hours per Patient Day vs. a target of 8.80.

EXERCISE 7.3 (Challenging)

7.3.1 Referring to Exhibit 7.1: What would be the difference, in Paid FTEs, if the Physical Therapy department had achieved an average of 95% on their Productivity Ratios over the last nine pay periods?

Answer: According to the report, the average Target Worked Hours was 711 and the average Actual Worked Hours was 805. The resulting Productivity Ratio was 88% (711 / 805). To achieve 95% of target, the department worked hours would have to approximate 748 (711 / 0.95).

Paid-to-Productive ratio for the nine periods = 893 / 805 = 1.11

Worked Hours difference = 748 - 711 = 37 Worked Hours

Paid Hours difference = 37 Worked Hours x 1.11 Paid-to-Productive ratio = 41 Paid Hours

41 Paid Hours / 80 Hours per Pay Period = **0.5 Paid FTEs**

7.3.2 Referring to Exhibit 7.1: If overtime hours were completely replaced by regular hours, what would be the annualized impact?

Answer: The productivity report shows the Overtime Premium for each pay period. This "premium" is computed as overtime expenses - overtime hours paid at average regular wage rates. Since the average overtime premium is reported as $347, the annualized impact would be:

$347 per pay period x 26 pay periods per year = **$9,022 per year**

7.3.3 Referring to Exhibit 7.5: Looking at the manager's daily sheet, what accounts for the difference between the estimated and actual results?

Answer: Actual census is based on a different measure than for each shift. The department was clearly staffed according to the grid. The staffing level was established based on each shift's patient census (demand).

However, unlike other departments where volumes for each shift are cumulative, nursing unit volumes are based on Patient Days which are determined by the midnight census. In this case, the midnight census was lower than patient volumes during the other two shifts. The midnight census was 21 and the average of the three shifts was 22.

If the midnight census had been 22, the actual HPPD would have been 8.36. Of course, this variation can go both ways...

7.3.4 Though the staffing grid is a planning tool, how can it also be effectively used for retrospective analysis?

Answer: Managers can review prior periods' grid reports, to assess responses to different levels and intensity of patient volumes, enabling them to improve their management skills and further refine the grid as a planning tool.

Notes

Notes

10. Appendix

Note: The information provided in this Appendix is for reference purposes and will not be used for any exercises. The two topics herein offer steps and insights for managers and senior managers that wish to take their benchmarking and peering efforts to a further level.

Typical Benchmarking Practice — Expanded

Most healthcare facilities use the most basic form of benchmarking to measure their departmental efficiency as compared to "peer" departments. The process includes:

1. Select a review time period. Generally a year is used in order to eliminate seasonal variances.

2. Collect actual department unit of service ("UOS") volumes. The units of service should correspond to those measured in the benchmarking database (refer to vendor documentation for details regarding definitions and what is included or excluded in the calculations). The UOS for most nursing departments will be "Patient Days", the Laboratory UOS will typically be "Billed Tests", etc.

3. Collect "Productive Hours."

    a. Include those hours designated "productive" by the benchmark database vendor. Again, by default, the major vendors consider Regular, Overtime, Education and Orientation time to be "Productive."

    b. Include payroll hours worked in the department. This is not as obvious as it sounds. Often, nursing staff will float to other departments. More often than not, they will clock in and out as appropriate. Most payroll systems collect hours worked and paid in both the "Home" department and the "Worked" department. For the purpose of benchmarking departmental labor productivity performance, you will want the data from the worked department.

c. Include contracted labor hours. The definition of contracted staff is simply "those paid to work in lieu of on-payroll employees." This includes registry and Traveler nurses, non-clinical temporary employees and outsourced management, often found in Dietary and Housekeeping. As these staff are paid for time worked, their numbers are the same for both worked and paid categories.

If you do not have hours for some contracted staff, such as a Dietary Manager, simply assign the number of hours for an FTE ("Full Time Equivalent") for the review period. If the review period is one year, an FTE would be 2080 hours (52 weeks x 40 hours per week). If less, an FTE would be calculated at 40 hours per week times the number of weeks in the review period.

4. Collect the number of Paid Hours for the period.

a. Calculate non-productive hours for department payroll staff. These include Vacation/Holiday/Sick time ("PTO" if combined), Jury and Bereavement leave, and other hospital designated non-productive time.

   i. Exclude hours associated with Call or Differential time.

   ii. If Overtime hours are tracked at the regular wage rate and the incremental (50% or more) rate, separately, only collect the number of hours for the regular component. Collecting both would be double counting. This is an unusual payroll approach, but happens enough to warrant mention herein.

b. Combine the productive hours from section 3 above (remember to include contract labor hours).

5. To determine departmental productivity for the review period, divide the number of productive hours (#3 above) by the unit of service volumes for the same period. The resulting "efficiency" measure will be in units of Productive Hours per Unit of Service (also referred to as Worked Hours per Unit of Service).

6. Compare and contrast the resulting productivity measure to peer department results at the top decile, top quartile and median of the benchmarking database.

7. To estimate the financial impact of achieving benchmarks, calculate the difference between total Actual Productive Hours and total Target Productive Hours (benchmark metric times associated unit of service volume). Next, convert the difference to Paid Hours. Finally, multiply the average departmental wage rate by the Paid Hours difference. Repeat for each of the benchmark percentiles you are comparing against.

    a. To adjust to Paid Hours, simply divide actual department Paid Hours by Productive Hours, for the review period, and multiply this "Paid-to-Productive ratio" by each Productive Hours difference figure.

    b. Apply the average Regular Wage rate, for each department, to the calculated Paid Hour differences.

        i. For conservatism's sake, use the department's average Regular Wage Rate. This excludes overtime, differential, call, one-time payments, etc.

8. Too may organizations stop at #7, selecting staffing standards that are equal, or relative, to these benchmarks. They point to the difference and tell their managers "Look at the gap! We need to close the gap!"

9. But this is the time for questions, not declarations. Questions such as:

    a. How are we different than our best performing peers?

    b. Why are we different than our best performing peers?

    c. Are we constrained from improving our staffing metrics due to:

    i.   State mandates

   ii. Administrative mandates

  iii. Significantly different patient demographics

  iv. Significantly different services

       1. Why are our services so different from our peers?

       2. Are we doing another department's work for them (perhaps thereby "subsidizing" their metrics)?

          a. Do we do it more efficiently and cost effectively than they would?

   v. Significantly different processes

       1. Why are they so different from our peers?

  vi. Dated technology

       1. What would the cost/benefit be from updating our technology?

 vii. Department's physical layout impacts our efficiency and effectiveness

       1. Can this be addressed cost-effectively?

Once the questions are answered, and the <u>justified differences</u> have been assessed for their measurable impact on efficiency ("justified" means they have survived the scrutiny and questions), the remaining difference from best practice peers must be addressed. The next step is to build an Action Plan, showing:

1) Adjusted Staffing Targets

2) What changes will be done to achieve those Targets

3) What date they will be completed by and

4) Who will be accountable for achieving the agreed-to targets.

Advanced Benchmarking Practice — Expanded

According to Michael J. Spendolini, author of "The Benchmarking Book", "*Benchmarking is a continuos, systematic process of evaluating the products, services, and work processes of organizations that are recognized as representing best practices for the purposes of organizational improvement.*" [4]

Many organizations pursue expanded benchmarking and peering practices to seek opportunities and steps to improve their quality, efficiency and effectiveness.

These organizations undertake a full, systematic, ongoing process of designating teams to

1) Investigate opportunities

2) Find best practice peers

3) Interview representatives of those peer hospitals and departments

4) Identify and implement process improvement opportunities

5) Monitor and evaluate improved processes

Teams can benchmark with identified "peers" at the organizational, departmental and even departmental process level. "Peers" do not have to be in the same industry! For example, hospital Admitting & Registration departments may benchmark certain admitting tasks against those of hotels, seeking opportunities to adopt best practices to improve specific processes within their own department. Best practices are identified through researched periodicals, peer phone interviews and even on-site visits.

Benchmarking performance measurement indicators must be:

1. Measurable

    a. Can you capture these measures readily?

    b. Are they to be weighted?

2. Comparable

    a. Are your peers measuring the same indicators?

    b. Are they measuring them in the same manner?

3. Equitable

    a. Does the measure really consider activities on the unit?

The most effective benchmarking teams are cross-functional — including external department representatives from client departments, feeder departments and support departments.

As Paul Fogel writes in his excellent book, "Superior Productivity in Health Care Organizations — How to Get it — How to Keep it", *"Benchmarking is aimed at learning what other organizations do, how they do it, and how this knowledge can be adapted and harnessed to work at one's own organization."*

Paul further notes, *"For benchmarking to be a success, managers have to be eager to do it, not have it imposed on them, which takes real teamwork and the sincere desire to improve."* [4]

Organizations that fully participate in benchmarking agree to abide by a "Partnering Code of Conduct"as their teams begin contacting peers.

PARTNERING CODE OF CONDUCT
Principle of Legality
Avoid discussions or actions that might lead to or imply an interest in collusion or restraint of trade. Do not discuss costs with competitors if costs are an element of pricing.
Principle of Exchange
Be willing to provide the same level of information that you request, in any benchmarking exchange.
Principle of Confidentiality
Treat benchmarking interchange as something confidential to the individuals and organizations involved. An organization's participation in a study should not be communicated externally without their permission.
Principle of Use
Use information obtained through benchmarking partnering only for the purpose of improvement of operations within the partnering companies themselves. External use or communication of a benchmarking partner's name with their data or observed practices requires permission of that partner.
Principle of First Party Contact
Initiate contacts, whenever possible, through a benchmarking contact designated by the partner company. Obtain mutual agreement with the contact on any hand off of communication or responsibility to other parties.
Principle of Third Party Contact
Obtain an individual's permission before providing their name in response to a contact request.
Principle of Preparation
Demonstrate commitment to the efficiency and effectiveness of the benchmarking process with adequate preparation at each process step; particularly, at initial partnering contact.
Source: SPI Benchmarking Code of Conduct

Notes

11. References

1   "Income, Poverty and Health Insurance Coverage in the United States: 2007", U.S. Census Bureau. Issued August 2008

2   "The Cost of Lack of Health Insurance", American College of Physicians White Paper, 2004

3   "The Uninsured: Access to Medical Care:, American College of Emergency Physicians website http://www.acep.org/patients.aspx?id=25932

4   Michael J. Spendolini, The Benchmarking Book, New York: AMACOM 1992

5   Paul Fogel, Superior Productivity in Health Care Organizations: How to Get It, How to Keep It, Health Professions Press: Baltimore 2004

Notes

Notes

Notes

Notes

About the Author

Keith Gott has more than twenty-five years of healthcare experience. He has supported comprehensive operational improvement and turnaround efforts at hospitals throughout the United States. He has expertise in process improvement, financial analysis, and labor productivity analysis with implementation for hospitals and multi-hospital systems.

Keith has been Vice President for Service Delivery at Quorum Health Resources, Associate Vice President at Cambio Health Solutions, Vice President and COO for Managed Care Resources, Senior Manager at MECON and a financial and operational manager for hospitals and medical groups.

He has led classes and seminars, teaching healthcare executives and department managers throughout the United States about Labor Productivity Management, and declares that he derives his greatest satisfaction therefrom.

As a Principal at Applied Health Sciences Consulting, Keith is responsible for ongoing client consulting and education services, project management for select consulting projects and clients and new business development.

View Keith's LinkedIn profile at http://www.linkedin.com/in/keithgott

Made in the USA
Lexington, KY
10 May 2011